Paul Martin

Paul Martin

A Political Biography

Robert Chodos, Rae Murphy, and Eric Hamovitch

James Lorimer & Company Ltd., Publishers
Toronto 1998

James Lorimer & Company Ltd. acknowledges the support of the Depart-ment of Canadian Heritage and the Ontario Arts Council in the development of writing and publishing in Canada. We acknowledge the support of the Canada Council for the Arts for our publishing program.

Every effort has been made to trace the ownership of all copyrighted material reproduced in this book. We regret any errors and will be pleased to make any necessary corrections in future editions.

Cover photograph: Canapress/Tom Hanson

Canadian Cataloguing in Publication Data

Chodos, Robert, 1947-
    Paul Martin

Includes index
ISBN 1-55028-628-5

1. Martin, Paul, 1938- 2. Canada-Politics and government-1993-.* 3. Cabi-net ministers-Canada-Biography.* 4. Politicians-Canada-Biography. 5. Businessmen-Canada-Biography. I. Hamovitch, Eric. II. Murphy, Rae, 1935-. III. Title

FC636.M37C46 1998   971.064'8'092   C98-932468-0
F1034.3M37C46 1998

James Lorimer & Company Ltd., Publishers
35 Britain Street
Toronto, Ontario
M5A 1R7

Printed and bound in Canada.

CONTENTS

Introduction   *1*

1   The Problems of the Father   *7*
2   Montreal Millionaire   *31*
3   The Road to Political Power   *60*
4   Slaying the Deficit Monster   *92*
5   A Dubious Legacy   *119*
6   Balancing Act   *135*

Note on Sources   *161*
Index   *165*

INTRODUCTION

Finance Minister Paul Martin is one of Canada's dominant public figures — perhaps *the* dominant one. With the government's agenda focused to an extraordinary extent on the elimination of the deficit, the finance minister has occupied centre stage. Martin has cast even his nominal leader, Jean Chrétien, into the shadows. And throughout Chrétien's first five years in office, Martin was often touted as his successor.

A number of factors have placed Martin at the centre of Canada's political life in the 1990s. First of all, as the son of a politician who served in the cabinets of four Liberal prime ministers, Martin has deep roots in the Liberal Party. Building on these roots, he has come to represent what the Liberal Party stands for in the 1990s — the strengths that keep it in power and the tensions and contradictions that it can never quite escape.

Second, most of Martin's adult life before he became a member of Parliament was spent in business, notably as president and owner of Canada Steamship Lines. As a result he incarnates the relationship between business and government that is an important part of politics in any era but is especially so in the 1990s. Managing that relationship has been a central element of Martin's career and has led to some of his most difficult moments.

Third, when he took on the finance portfolio, the seemingly impossible task of eliminating the federal deficit, which had proved more than a match for several of his predecessors, fell to him. To almost everyone's surprise, he accomplished what he set out to do, bringing the deficit down to zero in less than five years. In the process he thoroughly dominated Jean Chrétien's cabinet, with other ministers playing supporting roles at best.

Impressive as it is, Martin's achievement raises a number of questions. Why did the deficit disappear so quickly under his management? Why did a politician who had been critical of deficit reduction through spending cuts while in opposition adopt precisely this approach once in power? What other choices did he have? Has the struggle against the deficit had the economic benefits that its proponents promised? What was the social cost? How did Martin succeed in containing the political damage that spending cuts usually bring? And what will he do for an encore?

Paul Martin undoubtedly has his own answers to these questions. We would have liked him to share them with us, but despite several attempts, we were unable to set up an interview. Given the focus of our book, however, we have not been unduly hampered by this. As in our previous books, it was never our intention to write an insider's account. We were not able to — nor did we want to — match the blow-by-blow story of the struggle against the deficit provided by Edward Greenspon of the *Globe and Mail* and Anthony Wilson-Smith of *Maclean's* in their narrative of the Chrétien Liberals' first term in office, *Double Vision*. Greenspon and Wilson-Smith give Martin a co-starring role with the prime minister, and we have little to add to the specifics of their story, although our interpretation of some events differs from theirs.

It is as a public figure that Paul Martin is significant, and it is Martin the public figure who is our subject in this book. That said, we were fortunate to obtain interviews with a number of people who have worked with Martin in various capacities and know him well on both a personal and a professional level. The picture that emerged was of a decent and likeable individual — whatever one may think of his policies. A close personal friend describes Martin as being

> extremely passionate, a human kind of guy. He showed himself at Canada Steamship Lines to be just as comfortable talking to a deckhand as to the board of directors. He leads a lifestyle that is significantly below what his level of wealth would permit. He does not have flashy tastes. He doesn't wear anything flashy on his wrist or his neck. The cars he has driven are not posh, not a bank manager's cars. He loves to go down to his farm in the Eastern Townships on weekends and relax with his pals. He'll play a round of golf and eat hot dogs at the local golf club. He is really incredibly Canadian.

When Martin sought the Liberal leadership in 1990, *Globe and Mail* reporter Susan Delacourt asked, "How has such a seemingly unassuming man come to be assumed as the person best able to beat the powerful populist Jean Chrétien?" Certainly Martin does have personal qualities that have served him well: intelligence, a capacity for hard work, commitment to a task, a talent for communication, intellectual curiosity. Through these qualities, he became wealthy and powerful in the business world and then remarkably successful as a cabinet minister. But his life has not been filled with high drama, nor does it beg for deep psychological examination. He is essentially an ordinary person who has achieved extraordinary things.

Perhaps Martin's most surprising quality is his openness to a wide variety of ideas. He reads books by critics of the Liberal government such as Maude Barlow and Linda McQuaig. Greenspon and Wilson-Smith describe him as having been deeply affected by Jeremy Rifkin's apocalyptic critique of the effects of technology on employment, *The End of Work*. At other times he has been enthusiastic about the work of critical political economists such as James Tobin and Robert Reich. According to a close associate, he reads such books not simply to challenge them but to glean ideas that he might be able to assimilate into his own thinking.

Not heavily encumbered with ideology, Martin takes on a task and pursues it to the end. A friend describes him as energetic — "just being with him can make me feel tired" — and "very task-oriented. For him, getting something done is the greatest good. He thinks very much in terms of the tasks in front of him. He is solution-oriented. The question is always: How do we get there?"

For us, the question came down to: What choices did he have? If we are to be critical of Paul Martin for his single-minded concentration on the deficit and the approach he took to eliminating it, we need to know that there were realistic alternatives he could have pursued that would have led to a better result. The case for the existence of such alternatives is forcefully presented by Linda McQuaig in her recent book *The Cult of Impotence*. McQuaig writes,

> The obstacles preventing us from gaining control over our economic lives have little to do with globalization and technology. The real obstacle is political. Governments have backed off from taking action to fight unemployment and provide well-funded social programs not because they lack the means but because they've chosen to render themselves impotent, powerless in the face of capital markets. The technological imperative turns out to be mostly a failure of will on the part of governments.

A different picture was sketched for us by a senior Liberal adviser who is often portrayed as being on the progressive or "social" wing of the party. This adviser described the options facing the government as "marginal choices." If a more ideologically right-wing government had been in power in Ottawa instead of the Liberals, it might have cut social programs more deeply and rapidly; it might have reduced taxes; it might have allowed provincial premiers to do away with medicare, as several of them wanted to do. The Liberals may not have achieved much in a positive sense, but at least they prevented some negative things from happening.

In a context of increased sharing of sovereignty and rapid globalization of financial markets, this adviser emphasized the need for Canada to form alliances with other countries to give Ottawa more room to manoeuvre and provide a counterweight to the overwhelming power of the United States. There is much that could be done by governments acting together, but little that can be done by a single government acting alone. Manfred Bienefeld of Carleton University, who is highly critical of the Liberals, makes a similar point. To counteract the disproportionate and destructive power of the financial markets, he says, "What is needed is the cooperation of major governments. But this won't happen without a large-scale collapse."

We are inclined to agree with this view. Paul Martin was presented with an agenda that was not of his own making and over which he had little control, and he implemented that agenda very effectively. Interestingly, after declaring victory in his five-year battle with the deficit in February 1998, Martin took up a new theme. In his public speeches, he increasingly emphasized the need for effective international supervision of the global financial system. Addressing the annual Couchiching Conference in Orillia, Ontario, in August 1998, he noted that such supervision could have prevented the Asian crisis that has clouded economic prospects all over the world. If he is serious about pursuing this initiative, Martin will face obstacles that will dwarf those that stood in the way of a balanced budget. But if he succeeds, his achievement will create a far more substantial, and more clearly beneficial, legacy to Canada and to the world than the elimination of the deficit.

Martin's status as heir apparent to Chrétien is far from being a secure one. Even a cursory look at the history of leadership succession in Canada shows that early frontrunners face many pitfalls along the path to the top. Given his age (sixty at the time of writing) and his thorough identification with the painful struggle against the deficit, Martin faces more pitfalls than most. Deeply affected by having twice seen the Liberal leadership slip away from his father, in 1958 and 1968, he is acutely aware of the treacherous nature of the terrain ahead of him. We begin our account of Martin's life by looking at the highly political family in which he grew up and at the illustrious but ultimately frustrating career in government of Paul Martin, Sr.

CHAPTER ONE

The Problems of the Father

History doesn't repeat itself but it sure does rhyme.
Mark Twain

On January 20, 1948, William Lyon Mackenzie King rose to address a dinner in Ottawa's Château Laurier hotel marking a meeting of the National Liberal Federation. Here he announced that he would be retiring from public life. The forty-four-year-old minister of national health and welfare, Paul Martin, Sr., had been asked to speak at the banquet. He was flattered but was plainly worried. Worried for a number of reasons.

Martin's goal was the Liberal leadership — to be Canada's prime minister. As a Franco-Ontarian whose father read Wilfrid Laurier's parliamentary speeches to the family, he was a Liberal virtually from birth. He also was determined to enter politics from the day in 1919 when he stole away from the classical college he attended in Hull to witness Laurier's funeral procession through Ottawa: "Yes, as a young schoolboy I determined to strive to get into parliament and, like Laurier, aspired to be worthy of leading the Canadian people as prime minister. Theologians speak of vocations for the church; I believe there are vocations in public life as well."

As Martin adopted the Liberal Party, so also did the Liberal Party adopt the impecunious teenager as he advanced through universities in Canada, Britain and the United States. Through law school (a natural for the politically ambitious) and a lifelong interest in medieval philosophy and Catholic theology (less natural for a modern politician), young Martin was a Liberal stalwart and was regarded by much of the party elite as a comer.

After running unsuccessfully in a provincial election in his home town of Pembroke, Martin was elected federally in 1935 in his adopted riding of Essex East. This was a half-rural, half-urban constituency with a sizeable population of Franco-Ontarians, on the outskirts of Windsor, Ontario, where as a student he had worked in the Ford auto plant and at Windsor Raceway. Soon after his election, Martin met Nell Adams, who operated a family drugstore in Windsor. According to his own account, his courtship began when he first saw her as he bought a cigar from her. Flush with his new status as an MP, he was somewhat taken aback when she insisted she had never heard of him. Martin impulsively announced at that first meeting that he would marry her. More in character, he then procrastinated until she walked into his law office and announced that it was either now or never. They were married in 1936. Nell gave birth to a son, Paul, Jr., on August 28, 1938, and then a daughter, Mary-Ann, in 1944.

In the 1930s Windsor's fate was closely bound up with that of the auto industry, which employed some 65 per cent of the workforce. Even in Martin's semirural riding of Essex East there were thirty auto parts and accessories plants. Many thousands of Windsor residents also worked in auto plants across the river in Detroit — there was very little border supervision before the Second World War.

Windsor's most prominent politician was David Croll, who became mayor of Windsor in 1930 and went on to become a cabinet minister in the Liberal provincial government of Mitch Hepburn. As mayor he organized and led Windsor's welfare system, which didn't solve much since the city was particularly hard hit by the Depression. In 1937 Croll was dismissed from the cabinet by Hepburn after he supported the striking United Auto Workers in Oshawa and uttered the memorable line, "I would rather walk with the workers than ride with General Motors." He went back to Windsor and served as mayor again, and then went to Ottawa as a federal Liberal MP. In 1955 he was appointed to the Senate, missing out on a federal cabinet position only because he was Jewish. (It was left to another Windsor politician, Herb Gray, to become Canada's first Jewish federal cabinet minister in 1969.)

Windsor was also a leading centre of UAW organizing drives, and both Croll and Martin, who had good relations with the city's labour movement, supported the union. The two remained good friends and ideological soulmates through most of their careers. In the House of Commons, Martin spoke several times in favour of legislation that would guarantee the right to organize and have unions recognized, as did the 1935 Wagner Act in the United States. Mackenzie King's government did not act on such legislation until 1944, and the absence of such a legal framework made it difficult for industrial unions to organize in Canada during the thirties. In the forties the unions consolidated and the employers stopped resisting organization, expecting that after the war the returning veterans would smash the unions, as had happened in the aftermath of the previous war. The real showdown came in 1946, and although the strike movement was widespread, the most significant strike was probably at Ford in Windsor. As a local MP, Martin played a role in settling this strike, which led to the adoption of the historic Rand formula, according to which all members of the bargaining unit would pay dues and be covered by the agreement, whether or not they actually belonged to the union.

Despite his close labour ties, Martin was never a socialist, claiming that socialism was incompatible with his religion. Martin's labour ties were balanced by close links with wealthy Liberals such as Paul Nathanson, the reclusive head of the Famous Players theatre chain — a connection that would later have an echo in the political career of his son. But there was no incompatibility in Martin's mind between being a Liberal and being a friend of labour and a supporter of Franklin Roosevelt's New Deal, of which the Wagner Act was part. As a constituency politician he carefully tended his labour connections, and even maintained good relations with the Communists: He encouraged the division in the labour movement between the Communists and the CCF, from which the Liberals could only benefit.

Essex East, and indeed all of Windsor, became Martin's fiefdom. He worked the riding continuously, glad-handing and bestowing favours and gifts. The stories (many of them apocryphal) of his never-ending campaign are sprinkled through the memoirs of every Liberal politician of his day. A typical one is told in Christina McCall's *Grits*. Late in the afternoon of a day spent meeting and greeting his constituents, Martin came upon one local with, "Hello my good friend! How is your saintly mother today?"

"Same as she was this morning when you asked. Dead."

While he kept close watch on his constituency, Martin toiled on the backbenches in Ottawa for ten years after first being elected in 1935. He worked consistently for pensions, health insurance and every other aspect of the social policies the Liberal Party vigorously proclaimed and was traditionally so reluctant to advance. He also found time to keep his law practice, which included acting on behalf of the Dionne family, until Mackenzie King appointed him to the cabinet in 1945. The old leader was recruiting new blood for the postwar era, and Martin was one of a group of younger MPs elevated to cabinet rank, initially as secretary of state and then, a year and a half later, as minister of health and welfare.

Around this time, Paul, Jr., suffered a severe attack of polio (a disease from which Paul, Sr., had also suffered as a youth and which left him with a permanent if slight limp). In the immediate crisis, the boy was paralysed in the throat; after that passed his complete recovery took almost a year. However, by the time Paul, Jr., was in high school he was a member of the championship football team. He was a lively teenager with typical interests, more impressed with his father's meetings with prominent sports figures than with politicians and diplomats. By then the Martins were living in Ottawa, where Paul, Sr., had moved his family soon after his 1946 appointment to the health and welfare portfolio, a position he kept until the Liberals' defeat in 1957.

Politics was always a family project, and Nell played the role of supporter, advocate and promoter of her husband's career. In Martin's account, she was closer to Mackenzie King than he was. Indeed, she appeared to intimidate the prime minister — women did that, of course. Despite his Ottawa residence, Martin remained the constituency politician, taking the Thursday overnight from Ottawa to Toronto, the day train from Toronto to Windsor and back again to Ottawa Sunday night. On these visits he would stay at his in-laws' home, and he often brought his son and daughter along with him.

One can understand the son's pride in his father as they visited the constituency and the city itself where, as one family friend says, "Nobody passed Martin by without a smile or a handshake. Martin would go into a coffee shop and people would rise to give him their seat." And of course Martin reciprocated. In his memoirs Martin recalled his daughter Mary-Ann asking as a young child what Essex East was. Her impatient older brother interjected, "Don't you know? Essex East is the Holy Land." Later, in a high school debate, Paul, Jr.'s team successfully upheld the affirmative side of a resolution that Windsor was a better city than Ottawa — to his father's great satisfaction.

In the immediate postwar years Martin's duties expanded to include leadership of the Canadian delegation to the United Nations. On Thursday he would fly from New York to Ottawa, where he would work on Thursday and Friday. Then he would leave for Windsor on Saturday and fly back to New York on Monday. He was tireless. He was ambitious. And above all, he waited his turn.

Ambition and Disappointment

By early 1948, Mackenzie King's announcement that he was retiring was not unexpected. He had been in failing health for some time. And as his diaries were later to show, he was depressed and despondent about the course the postwar world was taking. His speech at the dinner on January 20, like most others of late, was a carefully constructed warning of the "Soviet menace" and the dangers posed by "World Communism." To himself and to his diaries, he confessed his own and his country's powerlessness to halt the slide towards the inevitable international crisis. At the same time he worried about Canada's fate and future in this impending conflagration.

King had agonized for months, perhaps years, as to whether he should resign or not. He had begun actively engaging in séances and various forums and mediums for communicating with the dead, conjuring up Franklin Roosevelt, Sir Wilfrid Laurier and others who, he claimed in his diary, pleaded with him not to resign. The image of Roosevelt is significant because it was the United States and its claims on Canada that alarmed King as much as anything in the threatening postwar world. In 1948 he secretly negotiated a free trade agreement with the United States only to scrap it, presumably at the behest of Laurier. More likely, it was Henry Luce and *Time* magazine, which proclaimed Canada the "49th state," that frightened King off and led him to try to revitalize (or, since it had never had much life, vitalize) the British Commonwealth.

In December 1947 — after an outburst in cabinet in which King denounced a decision to accept, at American behest, a position on a temporary United Nations mission to Korea — he recorded in his diary, "The more I think over, the more I believe … that the US foreign policy at bottom is to bring Canada into as many situations affecting themselves as possible with a view to leading ultimately to the annexation of our two countries." This outburst almost forced the resignation of King's designated successor, External Affairs Minister Louis Saint-Laurent. King always had a skeptical view of Canada's international entanglements. He was a lukewarm supporter of the United Nations, just as he had been of the League of Nations and the various other international agencies. Saint-Laurent, on the other hand, was an enthusiastic internationalist, or more precisely a selective internationalist in that he supported all things American — NATO and later NORAD. Thus, King's outburst over what everyone thought was a routine matter put Saint-Laurent in a very awkward position.

Paul Martin was a keen student of international affairs — an interest he would pass on to his son. Martin, Sr., supported most, if not all, multinational bodies, from the League of Nations in the 1920s and 1930s to the new United Nations and all its affiliates, especially the International Labour Organisation. This put him on thin ice with King, who was always suspicious of him. As minister of health and welfare he was not directly in King's line of fire, but he had earlier been warned. In his memoirs, Martin recalled a meeting he spoke at with King in the audience:

> I repeated my profession of independence, making it clear that above my party, I will place the interests of my country and my constituency and to this end I will speak my mind in parliament or out ... Some months later, when I was taking a pretty independent stand on foreign policy in the Commons, the prime minister took me aside and said, "Martin, I always remember that speech you made about being independent. Let me give you some advice. You can be too independent."

Martin also knew that his reputation in the party as a reformer — a social Liberal, a left Liberal — made him suspect in the eyes of the party establishment. He was a firm admirer of Franklin Delano Roosevelt and an avid supporter of the American New Deal. In his memoirs he spoke of his friendship with one of FDR's sons, and described how he contacted James Roosevelt from Windsor when he read that FDR would be campaigning in Detroit. Martin was surprised to be invited to breakfast, and even more surprised when his audience made the newspapers on both sides of the border. Along with Vincent Massey, Martin organized a conference in Port Hope in 1933 with a number of leading lights of the Roosevelt administration, who essentially came to lecture the boys on the efficacy of the New Deal for Canada. King, as leader of the opposition, was not amused. King never supported the New Deal and he sat in smug silence when R.B. Bennett sought to introduce aspects of Roosevelt's policies into Canada during the dying days of his government in 1935. As we have seen, it wasn't until 1944 that our enlightened friend of labour accepted a version of the famous Wagner Act which allowed the recognition of industrial unions. Martin also knew that his progressive bent would always leave him vulnerable with the new leader, Saint-Laurent, and his alter ego C.D. Howe.

That Louis Saint-Laurent was to succeed King had been apparent for a long time to the relatively young but very ambitious Paul Martin. He had one consolation, however, in that in 1948 he was one of the "under fifties" group in the cabinet — Douglas Abbott and Brooke Claxton were others — and over in External just-fifty Lester Pearson was ready to move into the portfolio when his mentor, Saint-Laurent, became prime minister. If Martin's luck and timing were good, and above all if he didn't alienate the new establishment, his turn could finally come.

Two Liberal traditions made Martin's task especially delicate. The first was the principle of French–English alternation in leadership, which was a relatively new tradition. Laurier had succeeded two hapless and unfortunate Liberal leaders from Upper Canada — Alexander Mackenzie, who left after his defeat by John A. Macdonald in 1878, and Edward Blake, who called it quits in 1887. When King succeeded Laurier in 1919, few delegates took into account that he was not a Quebecer. Rather, his loyalty to Laurier through the dark days of war and conscription had won him the support of Quebec delegates to a leadership convention when there were no candidates from Quebec.

The second Liberal tradition seeks to create and exploit a division within the party between left and right or between business Liberals and progressive or social Liberals. This division is more apparent than real, but it is obvious that the Liberal Party harbours very right-wing politicians and some left-leaning ones. And there are any number of gradations between the "extremes" — to use a very un-Liberal expression. They shift and realign, with age and ambition often affecting the mix. They also coexist and thus enable the party to campaign from the left and govern from the right, thus keeping its hold over the so-called mushy middle that has dominated the Canadian postwar electorate.

King's announced retirement in 1948, which brought Saint-Laurent to the centre of what little leadership speculation there was, also brought Paul Martin, the best known "social Liberal" in the cabinet, to the podium. The conventional wisdom of the time was that while Saint-Laurent was to be King's successor, at age sixty-six he would merely be an interim leader. As Canadian Press reporter Ross Munro noted about Saint-Laurent the next morning, "He probably would only fill the gap for a few years ... and there are aggressive young men in the cabinet coming ahead rapidly ... ministers with known ambitions for the long-term leadership." Prominent in Munro's list was Paul Martin.

Martin was chosen to give one of two "preliminary" addresses — along with the newly minted minister of veterans' affairs, Milton Gregg, a Victoria Cross winner. Gregg, who was not considered leadership material, said the party must support young people and help veterans. Since even temporary "gap-fillers" like Saint-Laurent tend not to keep aggressive and ambitious leadership hopefuls around, the ultra-careful Martin recognized that his speech had to reflect an exact tone. He had to please both King and Saint-Laurent as well as appeal to his constituency in the party. He did not want his speech to be seen as "closing doors and convincing some in the party that I was far too progressive ever to be considered Liberal leader."

Mackenzie King made his task more difficult by letting it be known that he was not about to become a lame duck. Only the day before he had shuffled his cabinet, and in his speech at the banquet he mused in his typically ambiguous fashion about how he wanted to retire — without actually announcing his retirement. He merely called for a leadership convention, leading at least one pundit to suggest that he might stand for reelection. Although that seemed far-fetched, King made one thing clear in his studied ambiguity: He was still in charge and he was keeping his options open.

Striking a note that would neither offend the old man nor appear to challenge his ordained successor, Martin stressed the "emphasis which liberalism has always placed on unity ... Its symbol is that with Baldwin there was a Lafontaine, with Laurier a Fielding; with King a Lapointe — and a Louis Saint-Laurent." It was a nice and delicate speech about this orderly transition and possibly the next, gently stroking his two leaders and assuring everybody that he would wait his turn and be faithful to the long and steady continuum of Liberal policy set over the years by William Lyon Mackenzie King.

Martin was confident that his turn would come soon enough. Even the final paragraph in Ross Munro's article did not give him too much cause for concern: "Finally, off in the wings of the civil service is L.B. Pearson, Under-Secretary of External Affairs. His name has come up from time to time, but it would be an extremely long shot for a senior civil servant to be drafted to the leadership despite his great abilities and personal magnetism." In August King resigned as party leader, although even then he kept his successor cooling his heels for three more months. On November 15, 1948, King finally turned his office over to Louis Saint-Laurent.

Who was to guess that the initially reluctant Saint-Laurent would like being prime minister? As an Anglophobe, he shared none of King's angst about American manifest destiny, and was among the most exuberant Cold Warriors of the time. He was devoted to NATO, which he considered his own project, helped design NORAD in the 1950s, and — most illustrative of all — broke with the British and French over Suez in 1956 and was the real author of Pearson's peacekeeping proposal. When not golfing with President Eisenhower he developed the avuncular Uncle Louis image. C.D. Howe — who had made a small fortune building grain elevators before entering politics in 1935, on the eve of his fiftieth birthday — was the cabinet's strongman, especially in all areas related to business and the economy, in some ways foreshadowing the role later played in Jean Chrétien's cabinet by Paul Martin, Jr. As Howe's biographers Robert Bothwell and William Kilbourn wrote,

> No one has been so successful in bringing together politics and business, using political power first to dominate and then to guide. His relation to Canada's big businessmen was indeed the most remarkable aspect of Howe's career. He was their leader, even though he did not come from their ranks.

Less senior ministers were expected to bend to his will. Howe initially admired Paul Martin, Sr.'s ambition and drive, but he did not approve of Martin's commitment to social spending. While Martin laboured in the neglected department of health and welfare through the early and middle 1950s (more than once he uttered the spoonerism "wealth and hellfire"), the cabinet as a whole operated as if it were the board of directors of Canada Ltd., under Saint-Laurent as chief executive officer and Howe as chief operating officer. And like a corporate board of directors, the government was not overly burdened with notions of democratic accountability. In the 1956 pipeline debate, the government's most arrogant and mean-spirited side was on full display. With Saint-Laurent and Howe both now in their seventies, the Liberals rammed straight ahead into the 1957 election, never considering the possibility of defeat. The voters had other ideas and elected a Conservative minority government under John Diefenbaker, bringing twenty-two years of Liberal rule to an end.

Saint-Laurent resigned soon after the election disaster, precipitating a leadership contest. Martin's contemporaries Brooke Claxton and Douglas Abbott had both left politics several years earlier, Claxton for the private sector and Abbott for the bench. With only Lester Pearson still around among his potential rivals for the leaderhip, Martin was convinced that his turn had at last arrived. But there is one Liberal tradition that, while deeply entrenched, is relatively undiscussed: when it is time to change leaders, the party seeks to find someone unsullied by the recent past — someone who carries as little baggage as possible. When King replaced Laurier, he had been out of Parliament since his defeat in 1911, and out of the country for a good part of that time. Saint-Laurent, who replaced King after only a few years in Parliament, was totally disconnected from the party's Quebec wing and was blameless in the 1942–44 conscription débâcle. In 1957 Lester Pearson was politically unsoiled, having missed most of the glare of the pipeline debate and other issues that brought the Liberals down. The announcement of his Nobel Peace Prize in the fall of that year gave him an aura that Martin could not match. Increasingly desperate, Martin went to — of all people — C.D. Howe to plead for support, arguing that only a francophone candidate such as himself could maintain good relations between Canada's founding peoples. Howe was unmoved. When the Liberals met in convention in January 1958, it was Pearson, 1,074 votes; Martin, 305.

From Left to Right to Irrelevance

Pearson, almost sixty, would not be around forever. Martin was five years younger and could still hope that his time would come. He was one of the few Liberal survivors of John Diefenbaker's sweep in March 1958 and became an effective opposition frontbencher. The political decade beginning with the

Diefenbaker landslide and ending with Pierre Trudeau's first election victory has been best described by the titles of Peter C. Newman's books: *Renegade in Power* and, more germane, *The Distemper of Our Times*. But through all the events of the Diefenbaker era, when Liberal giants fell like tenpins, and the Pearson minorities where the two-party system really began to crumble, Windsor and Paul Martin seemed unscathed.

Paul, Jr., was at university, with no strong personal inclination towards any particular career path. Rather, he pursued interests inherited from his father: philosophy at St. Michael's College in Toronto (which his father urged on him over his first tentative choice of political science), and then law at Osgoode Hall. He also inherited his father's Liberal partisanship and his interest in international affairs. When still in high school he got into trouble for stoning the Soviet Embassy, and while at St. Michael's he was active in young Liberal circles. Keith Davey recalls a messy Liberal rally at Massey Hall in Toronto that saw young Martin detained by police after a near-riot outside the hall.

But there was one respect in which Paul, Jr.'s life would be very different from his father's. Paul, Sr., was determined that his son would avoid his own lifelong financial worries. If the young man were to enter politics, it would be only after making his mark in some other field and establishing himself financially. And so in 1966, after graduating from Osgoode Hall, Paul, Jr., moved to Montreal to take a position with Power Corporation, embarking on a highly successful business career. In 1965 he had married Sheila Cowan, the daughter of his father's Windsor law partner, William Cowan.

As the Liberals settled into opposition after 1958, searching for a way back to power, the old tension between business and social Liberals resurfaced in a new context, and in the peculiar circumstances of those years the advantage appeared to be with the left. The issue was raised at the Kingston Conference in 1960, originally conceived as a smallish, informal "thinkers' retreat" to help develop a new electoral strategy. Most of the leading lights of the party were involved, the whole leadership endorsed the original concept of the conference, and Mitchell Sharp — later the leading business Liberal in Pearson's cabinet — issued the original invitations to attend. Pearson attended, as did Martin. According to Tom Kent, a key Liberal strategist, the motivation for reinventing the Liberal Party came from two sources. On one side, Diefenbaker's Tory government was unravelling. On the other, the Liberals felt threatened by the "New Party" then being formed out of an alliance of the CCF and the trade union movement — shortly to be officially dubbed the New Democratic Party.

Ever since the demise of the Liberal Party in Britain, it has been a given that in a parliamentary system based on constituency representation (rather than any variation of proportional representation) there can be only two national parties. Thus, in the long term, leaders of both the NDP and the Liberal Party have believed that one must die so the other can live. In Canada this equation is complicated by the highly regionalized nature of Canadian politics. The real challenge for a political party in Canada is not to achieve ideological unity but to achieve unity among the regions, and this can only be done by the most skittish of ideological politics. The New Party was moving away from the democratic socialist roots of the CCF to a more "moderate" stance. It appeared to the deep thinkers in the Liberal Party that the challenge the New Party represented was to the Liberal alternative, not to the Conservative government. To illustrate this, Kent describes an incident at the Kingston Conference. Speaking of a paper he presented, Kent says:

> The most immediately significant reaction was that of William Mahoney, Canadian National Director of the Steelworkers. ... [He] amended his prepared text to praise my paper and say, "If the Liberal Party ... comes up with a policy that implements the program outlined by Mr. Kent, this could well be the place where the aims of organized labour and the aims of the Liberal Party

could coincide." ... Walter Gordon was more forthright ... "I must shake the hand that has strangled the New Party before it was born."

Paul Martin, on the other hand, considered Kent's paper "half-baked." He was rather disdainful of the conference as a whole; some of the papers, he felt, "contradicted Liberal policy." Having carried the torch of social Liberalism through the Saint-Laurent years, Martin was not part of the reinvention of the Liberal Party in the early 1960s; it was a new group — Gordon, Kent, Keith Davey — that took the lead. In any case, this new progressive outlook, the harmony among the various wings of the party, and Paul Martin's social Liberalism all became severely tattered once the Liberals were returned to office under Pearson's leadership in 1963.

The tension took the form of an ongoing series of battles between Mitchell Sharp and Walter Gordon, which took place in cabinet when Gordon was a member (1963–65 and 1967–68), and in party meetings and through speeches and books, mainly by Gordon, when he was out. Gordon had the upper hand in the war of words, but Sharp easily won all the power struggles. These battles ranged over basic issues in Canadian domestic, foreign and economic policy, from medicare to free trade to foreign economic control.

Gordon's first budget in 1963, which proposed a tax to discourage American investment in Canada, collapsed not because a majority of Canadian would-be sellers and American buyers were upset (although they were) but because Canada needed American investment. When the Kennedy administration in Washington proposed a measure that would have had essentially the same effect a short time later, Gordon flew to Washington to beg them to exempt Canada.

Kennedy relented and so did Johnson, but Nixon would not listen to Canada and neither would Carter. There seemed nothing left to do but deal with Reagan on their terms — which

Canada subsequently did. Thus were born the free trade negotiations.

Another major issue involved American efforts to break into the
Canadian banking monopoly through the Rockefeller-controlled
Citibank's takeover of the Mercantile Bank of Canada. While the
issue was largely unresolved at the time, it will be finally
settled in a different context during Paul Martin, Jr.'s watch on
the ramparts (see chapter 6).

Paul Martin, Sr., now minister of external affairs, was almost
completely uninvolved in the struggles. In his memoirs Gordon
gives two lists of cabinet ministers — one of ministers who
typically supported him on issues under discussion and one of
ministers who typically opposed him. Martin's name is con-
spicuous by its absence from both lists. In External, Martin
worked to repair the "special relationship" with the United
States that had been strained by the actions of the Diefenbaker
government and then by Gordon's budget. In January 1965
Pearson and Martin travelled to the LBJ Ranch in Texas to sign
the Auto Pact — no small matter for a Windsor politician.
Repairing the special relationship also involved Canadian support for the Americans' escalating war effort in Vietnam, a task
the external affairs minister took on with enthusiasm. Martin
argued in cabinet that "while Canada had no intention of participating directly in Vietnam, she could not adopt the position
of being the only close ally of the United States to withdraw
her support."

At the same time, however, Martin still harboured vivid
memories of having his leadership campaign cut off at the
knees by Pearson's Nobel Peace Prize in 1957, and so was
keenly aware of the domestic political value of peace initiatives. In 1966 he conceived the notion of sending respected
diplomat Chester Ronning to Hanoi to arrange direct talks
between North Vietnam and the United States. A hesitant Ronning
met with Martin's deputy minister, Marcel Cadieux, who
insisted that he had to undertake the mission. Otherwise, as
Ronning later described the conversation, "Paul Martin

wouldn't be reelected in his constituency. I told him I wouldn't pull anyone's political chestnuts out of the fire. Cadieux again said Martin needed it for his constituency." In the end Ronning did go, and the North Vietnamese offered what appeared to be an important concession, but the Americans, who were suspicious of the initiative from the start, dismissed it as a ploy. The mission came to naught and the war continued to escalate.

In May 1967 Walter Gordon — recently reappointed to the cabinet after a year on the back benches — spoke out strongly against American policy in Vietnam, maintaining that the U.S. "has become enmeshed in a bloody civil war in Vietnam which cannot be justified on either moral or strategic grounds." Martin tried to line up support in cabinet to have Gordon fired. However, public reaction to Gordon's remarks was favourable, and the government — and especially Martin, with the next leadership campaign very much on his mind — began to change their tune on Vietnam. At a NATO foreign ministers' meeting in Luxembourg in June, Martin urged that the United States stop bombing North Vietnam. Gordon, whom Martin had brought with him, described it as an "excellent presentation" that "took courage."

Through his career, Paul Martin, Sr., moved from left to right to irrelevance without missing a beat or losing his seat in Parliament and the cabinet. He never changed his beliefs or his social conscience; he just prioritized his goals.

The Lessons of Defeat

As the senior minister in Pearson's feckless governments, which somehow seemed always on the verge of self-destruction, Paul Martin was seen, especially by himself, as Pearson's logical successor. He played his part almost perfectly, something like an Anthony Eden to Winston Churchill. The difference is that until his senility was obvious, Churchill was considered a strong prime minister and Eden his loyal protégé. The Pearson–Martin relationship was nothing of the sort, nor was it regarded as desirable, creditable or even possible for

Pearson's successor to be seen as continuing in footsteps so many of which had been missteps. A further complication was the perceived need for the next federal prime minister to deal with the demands and expectations unleashed by Quebec's "Quiet Revolution," a task for which Paul Martin was by every measure unqualified.

By early 1967, it was widely believed that Pearson would retire within the next year, and potential successors — especially Martin, Sharp, Paul Hellyer, Allan MacEachen and John Turner — began gearing up their leadership campaigns. During the summer Martin was in perhaps the most advantageous position, reaping the benefit of repeated opportunities to greet foreign dignitaries arriving at Montreal's Expo 67. In September the Conservatives chose a new leader, Nova Scotia Premier Robert Stanfield, and immediately opened up a substantial lead over the Liberals in the polls. There is perhaps no better comment on the state of Canadian politics at the time than the sense people briefly had that Stanfield represented the voice of a new generation. In a private memo in October, Walter Gordon noted that "there is no consensus in the Party as to the best man to succeed Mr. Pearson, although Paul Martin's support is greater than that of any of the others." To the extent that the Liberals — rank and file and leaders — saw Martin as a leading candidate to succeed Pearson, it was probably more as a caretaker who could take the party into opposition after Stanfield won his apparently inevitable victory.

In December Pearson finally announced his resignation and the contest was on in earnest. To manage his campaign, Martin brought in his son, twenty-nine-year-old Paul, Jr., who took a six-month leave from his job with Power Corporation in Montreal. Over the next few months the younger Martin, who ran the campaign with what his father later described as "remarkable zeal and loyalty," received a privileged political education in the workings of the Liberal Party and the ways in which it met the challenge it faced.

A number of myths grew up around the 1967–68 Liberal leadership campaign and the resultant "Trudeaumania," obscuring the real lessons a keen observer and aspiring politician such as Paul Martin, Jr., would have learned. One of these myths is the notion that Trudeau was at first reluctant to become leader: According to one popular history, he did not even actively seek the leadership once he was in the race. Another myth surrounding the campaign is that Trudeau was the choice of the rank and file of the party and forced on the reluctant power brokers. It is very hard to distinguish the rank and file from the power brokers — especially at a leadership convention where there may be more ex-officio delegates than elected constituency delegates and where, in any case, most of the constituency delegates are aspirant candidates and patronage recipients. In other words, as in any army, the rank and file take their marching orders from the officers and a disciplined political party such as the Liberals is such an army. Almost anybody can run for leader, at any level, but nobody can win without the blessing of the party leadership.

Another aspect of this myth was the perception that Paul Martin was the insider with the insider's track to the money and power of the party elite. But Martin — as his memoirs attest — did not have the backing of the party leadership. Indeed, he was specifically told not to contest the leadership by the leader himself. Martin's resulting humiliation was the consequence of his defiance. And so young Martin was left to see his father helpless as his delegates slipped away and the IOUs he had earned over forty years of service to the party were shredded.

Trudeau, unknown in the party, was thrust into prominence by Lester Pearson, first as his parliamentary assistant and then as minister of justice. He was given that portfolio at the moment when the Criminal Code was being revised. And Trudeau shone as the minister who took a line from a Toronto *Globe and Mail* editorial and announced that "the state has no business in the bedrooms of the nation." He went on from there to the high ground (at least it was then) of the constitution and his showdown with Quebec Premier Daniel (Equality or Independence) Johnson.

Once Jean Marchand declined, Trudeau was the only minister who could emerge as the Quebec candidate — here the principle of alternation comes into play. Pearson knew this and thus gave Trudeau the plum assignments and the national platform. Trudeau, while denying his candidacy, eagerly and carefully used this opportunity to improve his standing with the grassroots but more importantly to win over the party power brokers. Pearson told Trudeau that he would approve of him as a successor and would convey that feeling to his friends. Stephen Clarkson and Christina McCall describe a meeting between Trudeau and Jean de Grandpré, then vice-president of Bell Canada and a Liberal power in Quebec, before Trudeau announced his candidacy. De Grandpré, solidly on the party's right, warned Trudeau not to run. Trudeau listened carefully.

> But his response was strong and clear. If he did not run … he would be denying the validity of everything he had written about French Canadians being responsible for their own powerlessness because of their unwillingness to take full part in governing the Canadian federation.

This hardly sounds like a reluctant candidate, or one who was not trying to win over the party establishment in preparation for a leadership campaign he was determined to win. The race was to be a vindication of his vision of Canada — something he took very seriously indeed. This determination was reflected in the vicious internal struggle that marked the campaign — even with Pearson overtly helping him and "Trudeaumania" supposedly sweeping the country, Trudeau won the leadership by a handful of votes on the fourth ballot. The group that was most resistant to Trudeau's charms and that came close to preventing his victory consisted of the hard-core ideological knuckle-draggers who were insistent on moving the party to the right. This group coalesced around Robert Winters, the minister of trade and commerce and former head of the Brinco power company who had first entered the cabinet in the 1940s as a protégé of C.D. Howe.

But aside from the Winters effort, when final choices were being made business Liberalism and social Liberalism proved to be irrelevant — that was another lesson of the campaign. Walter Gordon supported Trudeau — who was clearly neither social nor business nor any other kind of a Liberal — because he thought it was a Quebecer's turn. Mitchell Sharp made a deal to support Trudeau after the wheels fell off his own campaign (rumour has it that Sharp had no support and could deliver none, but how was Trudeau to know?). And a number of prominent Liberals identified with the party's left, such as Judy LaMarsh and Keith Davey, ended up supporting the campaign of Paul Hellyer, politically quirky but generally identified with the party's right. (Davey switched to Trudeau after it became clear that Hellyer would not win, but LaMarsh switched to Winters. She retired from politics and later wrote a political *roman à clef* featuring the Silver Seven, the party establishment who tell prime ministers when to resign and anoint their successors.)

As for the candidacy of Paul Martin, the only place where it aroused any enthusiasm was his still faithful satrapy of Windsor. A journalist who attended a graduate seminar at the University of Windsor as a guest a few weeks before the convention recalls that all the talk was about Martin and whether anyone could mount a serious threat to his victory. The mention of Trudeau brought forward only uncomprehending stares. But beyond Windsor, where all seemed well in the Liberal universe, there was a sense of panic and Liberals felt almost unanimously that their political universe must unfold in a completely different way — a way that did not include Paul Martin. Even Martin's old friend David Croll was in the Trudeau camp.

Nevertheless, Paul, Jr., and the rest of the Martin campaign workers were shocked by the brutality of the first ballot, which gave Martin only 277 votes, behind Trudeau, Hellyer and Winters, and tied with John Turner. Martin quickly withdrew, declining to throw what remained of his support to any of the other candidates. Father and son later had different memories of Paul, Jr.'s reaction to the sudden and cruel end of the Martin campaign. "He took the defeat pretty hard — much harder than I," Paul, Sr., told reporter David Olive in 1984. "He didn't want to see his father get hurt." But Paul, Jr., said, "I felt no sense of betrayal, although I did feel badly for my dad."

Trudeau went on to defeat Winters and Turner on the final ballot. A final lesson of the campaign was that the Liberal tradition of always looking for the outsider, for the aspiring leader with the most tenuous connections with the old regime, was alive and well. Faithfully awaiting one's turn is not an option. As Martin noted in an uncharacteristically bitter passage in his memoirs,

In 1941 before Louis St. Laurent had become a member of the House of Commons — at fifty-nine — Mackenzie King invited him to join his government as minister of justice. The fifty-one year old Mike Pearson entered the cabinet the same way at the behest of St. Laurent and King. Pierre Trudeau came into the House of Commons when he was forty-six and entered the cabinet eighteen months later, at Pearson's request. The candidate who enters politics in this way is generally presented with an uncontested nomination and often with a fairly safe seat. Those who enter the cabinet from outside politics in some respects take advantage of the hard work of others and cash in on that work to obtain the victory that generally ensues.

Paul, Jr., returned to Montreal and resumed his climb up the corporate ladder, eventually becoming the owner of a major company and acquiring a personal fortune valued in the tens of millions of dollars. Unlike his father, he would not be burdened by personal financial constraints. Through it all he kept his Liberal connection well polished and contemplated an eventual return to political life. He had learned from Paul, Sr.'s humiliation that his best way to the top was not to wait his turn in the party ranks but rather to make his mark in another field of endeavour.

But no matter how well the son absorbed the lessons he learned from his father, both about what to do and about what not to do, there would be uncanny parallels in the political careers of the two Paul Martins. As happened with his father, Paul, Jr.'s first shot at the Liberal leadership would come too early, at a time when the party establishment was firmly behind another candidate. He would then serve as the senior minister and heir apparent in the cabinet of the politician who had defeated him. And, as happened with his father in 1968, Paul, Jr.'s next and last opportunity to seek the Liberal leadership may come too late.

Passing the Torch

Once Trudeau became prime minister, Paul Martin, Sr., had to vacate external affairs to make room for Sharp, to whom the new leader owed his victory, at least in part. Trudeau reportedly offered Martin the justice portfolio but he turned it down and instead became government leader in the Senate, accepting this position on the advice of his old friend Paul Nathanson of Famous Players. He stayed in the Senate for seven years, and then — by this time in his mid-seventies — he went to London as Canada's high commissioner.

After his return he wrote his voluminous memoirs, whose publication was financed by his wealthy son. He lived on to see Paul, Jr., nominated and then elected to the House of Commons in 1988 and was in his son's box when the younger Martin ran second to Jean Chrétien at the 1990 Liberal leadership convention. He died at the age of eighty-nine in September

1992, a little more than a year before his son succeeded to a place at the cabinet table where he had sat longer than anyone since Mackenzie King.

CHAPTER TWO

Montreal Millionaire

Paul Martin, Jr.'s active business career spanned twenty-three years and centred on just three individuals and two companies. The individuals were Maurice Strong, Paul Desmarais and Laurence Pathy, and the companies were Power Corporation of Canada and Canada Steamship Lines, which to this day share the same head office building facing Victoria Square at the edge of Old Montreal. Both are fabled companies with deep roots in the heart of the Canadian economy. Neither holds the weight or influence it once did, but both are still substantial entities, Power Corporation in insurance, mutual funds, overseas banking and publishing, Canada Steamship Lines in shipping on the Great Lakes and the St. Lawrence and, to a lesser degree, in European service.

The Power Connection

On March 1, 1966, Paul Martin began work at Power Corporation in Montreal, then still a dynamic business centre and the equal of Toronto as a hub of finance and corporate decision-making. Before the 1970s, it was not uncommon for Canadians from outside Quebec to settle in Montreal to promote their careers. The Martins bought a house on Wicksteed Avenue in the Town of Mount Royal, a comfortable upper-middle-class

suburb that nevertheless doesn't have quite the cachet of Westmount or upper Outremont.

Power Corporation was a place for ambitious young people
on the make, often with strong political connections or political
careers lying ahead. Many people with Power Corporation ties
have had a significant hand in Canadian politics in the last three
decades, both publicly and behind the scenes. Their ranks include Maurice Sauvé and Jean-Luc Pépin, federal Liberal cabinet ministers in the 1960s and 1970s; John Rae, Liberal
backroom boy and occasional adviser to Jean Chrétien (and
brother of former Ontario premier Bob Rae, a New Democrat);
and Daniel Johnson, senior cabinet minister under the late
Quebec premier Robert Bourassa, briefly premier himself in
1994 and leader of the Quebec Liberal Party until 1998. Links
with political power extend right into the family of longtime
Power chair Paul Desmarais, one of whose sons married Jean
Chrétien's daughter. Power's political links have lain predominantly, but by no means exclusively, with Liberals.
Louis Desmarais, Paul's brother and vice-chair of Power, got on
the phone with other corporate leaders to help Brian Mulroney
finance his brassy 1976 bid for the federal Progressive Conservative leadership. After that bid failed, Mulroney returned
to his labour law practice, where his clients in the late 1970s
included Power subsidiary Canada Steamship Lines.

At the time of Martin's arrival, the most prominent of
Power Corporation's entrepreneur-politicians was the company president, Maurice Strong, then in his late thirties. Strong
has had a long, varied and sometimes chequered career that has
taken him in and out of a bewildering array of businesses and
international organizations as well as into the top circles of the
federal Liberal Party, for which he once almost ran as a candidate during the Trudeau era. Combining a drive for business
success with a genuine interest in international development
and especially the environment, he has been secretary-general
of major United Nations conferences on the environment in
1972 and 1992; founding president of Petro-Canada, the pub-

licly owned oil company established by the Trudeau government in the 1970s; and chair of Ontario Hydro while Bob Rae
was premier in the early 1990s.

The story goes that, in 1943, the fourteen-year-old Strong,
having skipped four grades and graduated from high school,
arrived at Fort William (now part of Thunder Bay) looking for
work. The Canada Steamship Lines vessel *Noronic* was in port
and he stowed away, presenting himself to the second steward
to ask for a job after the ship had departed. He became a kitchen
assistant. A few years later he showed up at the newly founded
United Nations and landed a job there, but soon left to take a
position with the Winnipeg brokerage house James Richardson
and Sons. His next stop was the Alberta oil fields, where he
helped create the company that later became Dome Petroleum.

By the early sixties Strong was president of Power Corporation, then in a period of transition. Power Corporation of
Canada was created, in 1925, almost as an extension of investment dealers Nesbitt, Thomson and Company Limited. The
firm's two principals, A.J. Nesbitt and P.A. Thomson, served
in turn as presidents of Power from 1925 to 1956. As the name
suggests, Power Corporation invested in Canadian electric
utilities, in particular hydroelectric producers in Quebec. On
Thomson's death in 1956 the role of Power's professional
managers became more important, and it was in this period that
Strong emerged as a major figure in the company, becoming
executive vice-president in 1961 and president in 1963.

In 1963, Hydro-Québec took over most privately owned
electricity generating facilities in the province, leaving Power
Corporation sitting on a large pile of cash. When Power turned
its gaze to new acquisitions, Canada Steamship Lines was one
of the companies that came into sight. Algoma Steel Company
held 50 per cent of the shares and needed funds to finance an
ambitious expansion program. It sold about half its CSL holding to Power. This created no immediate alarm at CSL, because
Power had often been content with minority stakes in the companies in which it invested. But then Power made an immediate

demand for four seats on the CSL board of directors, which it filled with four of its top people, including Strong, as well as a position on the CSL executive committee, which Strong occupied.

Strong was already acquainted with the young Paul Martin, although their first encounter did not take a happy turn. During his stint in the Alberta oil industry, Strong established his own company, M.F. Strong Management Limited, which won a management contract with Ajax Petroleums Limited. Strong helped reorganize Ajax to form Canadian Industrial Gas Limited, later to become part of Norcen Energy Resources Limited. At age eighteen, Martin held a summer job as a roustabout, driving around the gas fields to check gauges on pumping equipment. One weekend he played hooky, taking a company truck to see the Stampede in Calgary. While he was on his way back to the gas fields, the truck ran into a ditch and overturned. This led to his firing — by company boss Maurice Strong. Later summer jobs found Martin as a deckhand aboard vessels in the Arctic, giving him his first direct exposure to the shipping industry.

Late in 1965, after completing his law degree and passing his Ontario bar exams, Martin was appointed to a job in Luxembourg with the legal branch of the European Coal and Steel Community, a precursor to the European Union. At this point, he was still uncertain as to what direction he wanted his career to take. Working for an international organization in Third World development held a certain allure for him, but things changed as the result of a chance encounter with Maurice Strong, who had apparently forgiven Martin for his youthful breach of responsibility in the Alberta gas fields. Strong urged him to broaden his background and obtain experience in business, which would allow him to make a more valuable contribution in any future Third World work. To ease Martin's decision, Strong offered him a job then and there as his special assistant at Power Corporation.

Corporate Firefighter

Strong left Power Corporation within seven months of Martin's arrival, but Martin stayed on, rising to become a vice-president in 1969. This rapid ascent took place despite — or perhaps because of — the six-month leave of absence he took in 1968 to help manage his father's campaign for the federal Liberal leadership, just as Paul Desmarais arrived on the scene at Power. With Desmarais at the helm, Power was a company where mixing business with politics, especially Liberal politics, was hardly a sin.

Born in 1927, Paul Desmarais had begun to amass a business empire out of the tattered remains of his father's near-bankrupt local bus company in Sudbury. After the company's fortunes improved, Desmarais began acquiring other bus lines, culminating in 1960 with the buyout of Provincial Transport Limited in Quebec and its Ontario sister company Colonial Coach Lines, both owned by the Drury family of Westmount (Bud Drury would soon become a Liberal MP and cabinet minister). In the next eight years, Desmarais, along with his brother Louis and his lieutenant Jean Parisien (both of them accountants), employed creative financial techniques to build a varied conglomerate named Trans-Canada Corporation Fund, with interests ranging from insurance to newspapers to racetracks. Desmarais became master of the reverse takeover, selling holdings to a bigger company in return for a block of shares that gave him effective control of the combined entity.

In 1968 Peter N. Thomson, chair of Power Corporation and son of the cofounder, proposed a merger with Trans-Canada under the Power aegis. Under this deal each component would hold equal voting rights, with Thomson as chair and Desmarais as chief executive officer. Desmarais used this position to establish his dominance. The result was an effective takeover of Power Corporation, with Thomson, who had never shown much enthusiasm for day-to-day management, quickly fading into the background.

One of Desmarais's first projects in his new position was to complete Power's takeover of Canada Steamship Lines. As Montreal historian Edgar Andrew Collard noted in *Passage to the Sea*, his narrative of CSL, "He wanted not just control, but total ownership." He bought shares on the open market, as well as a block belonging to financier J.W. McConnell, proprietor of the Montreal *Star*. He also employed a variation of the reverse takeover technique, selling Provincial Transport (by this time renamed Voyageur Enterprises) to CSL at market value in exchange for cash and enough shares to give Power clear majorities of both common and preferred shares. In 1971 and 1972, Power offered to buy all CSL common shares it did not already own at a substantial premium over the market price. This offer was accepted. Collard remarked, "Through a series of complex transactions Power had now been able to reap the tax benefits of using CSL's large pre-tax profits to absorb Power's own overhead and the interest costs arising from its various acquisitions. In this way CSL was to pay for itself." Acquisition of the remaining preferred shares was completed in 1975.

Paul Desmarais's ambitions did not end with Canada Steamship Lines. His buying spree left him sitting atop an empire that included — in addition to CSL and its trucking, bus and shipbuilding subsidiaries — paper-maker Consolidated-Bathurst, Dominion Glass, Investors' Group (then the dominant firm in Canadian mutual funds), Montreal Trust, Great-West Life, Laurentide Financial Corporation, Imperial Life, and a newspaper group with Montreal's *La Presse* as its flagship. Within this growing empire, Paul Martin acquired varied experience that prepared him for running a business empire of his own.

Early on, Martin caught the eye of Paul Desmarais, who admired his talent for dealing with troubled situations. Despite his relative lack of business experience, Martin became a sort of corporate firefighter, sent to various subsidiaries and divisions that needed an injection of management skill. This led to stints at Dominion Glass and then Consolidated-Bathurst, where he held the title of vice-president for special projects starting in 1971. Working with Consolidated-Bathurst president William Turner, a veteran Power executive, he took on the role of slasher, closing several mills and taking an axe to the payroll, especially at the management level. The formerly money-losing paper-maker was showing a profit when Martin left in 1973.

From there he went to CSL's Davie Shipbuilding division, which was reeling under the effects of a long drought of orders and then of a contract to build three 80,000-tonne tankers for a Greek shipowner that went badly wrong. At the time these were the largest vessels ever built by a Canadian shipyard. The company soon discovered that dealing with foreign customers, something in which it had little recent experience, was very different from the cosy world of Canadian shipping, where shipowners were less demanding and assurances of good faith on both sides seemed more than adequate. The Greek contract was very exacting in its detail and carried heavy penalties for late delivery. Serious problems developed and work fell far behind schedule, grinding almost to a halt at one point in 1972. Takis Veliotis, Davie's longtime general manager, bailed out, taking three of his key assistants with him.

Davie was also hurt by weak productivity and a poor labour relations climate. The workers' union, affiliated with Quebec's militant Confederation of National Trade Unions, took the approach that an owner with the deep pockets of Power Corporation could afford to meet high wage demands even if the shipyard itself was in poor financial shape. Power Corporation brought in new management at Davie, completed the Greek tanker contract at a heavy loss, and obtained orders for six new ships, aided by federal subsidies. However, costs of labour and materials were soaring far beyond expectations.

Despite the difficult situation Martin saw at Davie, it whetted his enthusiasm for the shipping industry. Late in 1973 Paul Desmarais appointed him president of Canada Steamship

Lines. In this position he replaced Louis Desmarais, who remained chief executive officer for another two years until Martin took on that title as well. "The appointment of Martin was very satisfactory to Paul Desmarais," Collard noted. "In Martin he was appointing not an unpredictable outsider but someone with whom he was well acquainted and whose abilities he had tested within Power in different situations." In harmony with his rise at Canada Steamship Lines, Martin also moved up in Montreal society, trading his Town of Mount Royal address for a much grander house on Belvedere Circle near the pinnacle of Westmount.

Canada Steamship Lines: The Legacy

From 1973 onward, Paul Martin held within his hands the destiny of a fabled piece of Canadian business history, first as president, then as half-owner, and later as full owner. For more than a century, CSL and its predecessors had been participants in many of the triumphs and also some of the more dubious episodes in Canadian shipping.

Although it was not created until 1913, Canada Steamship Lines brought together several smaller shipping lines, operating primarily on the St. Lawrence and the Great Lakes, with roots going well back into the nineteenth century. CSL was formed under Canadian management but with effective control exercised by a committee of London financiers. This was an era of mergers and consolidations in many industries, and developments in shipping were part of this pattern.

The biggest and oldest of the constituent lines that formed CSL was the Richelieu and Ontario Navigation Company, itself the product of a merger. The R&O's main component was La Compagnie du Richelieu, founded in 1845 by Jacques Sincennes, a merchant in Sorel at the confluence of the Richelieu and St. Lawrence rivers. Sincennes took advantage of a newly built canal that bypassed the rapids along the Richelieu near Chambly, and the company at first served farmers in the Richelieu valley seeking to bring their crops to Montreal. When this business was undermined by the arrival of the railways, La Compagnie astutely moved its boats entirely to the St. Lawrence, where it thrived despite intense competition and attempts to force it out of business or into mergers. Tales were told of steamships from rival companies racing each other recklessly along the river between Quebec and Montreal in the 1850s, each aiming to be the first to lower its gangplank at the port of arrival. This continued until a calamity in 1857 that cost 253 lives.

La Compagnie absorbed competitors and managed to maintain its independence, but finally yielded in 1874 under pressure from Sir Hugh Allan, who had built one of the dominant ocean lines of the time and who sought control over inland shipping to add to his other varied business interests. After some resistance, Sir Hugh was able to muscle La Compagnie du Richelieu into a merger with his Great Lakes–based Canadian Steam Navigation Company, forming the R&O. The new company performed poorly, however, and Sir Hugh's appointed directors were ousted in 1882 by unhappy shareholders. After a long period of uncertainty, the company was brought into firm hands again in 1895 with the arrival as president of Louis-Joseph Forget, a leading Montreal financier. Forget succeeded in attracting record numbers of passengers by ordering bigger, more luxurious ships, including vessels of shallow draught that could shoot the rapids of the upper St. Lawrence, and by developing resort hotels along the lower St. Lawrence.

Some time later, an unassuming Canadian dealmaker named Grant Morden, who had the ear of British capitalists, arrived on the scene and led a vigorous new round of consolidation in the inland shipping industry. Morden managed to enlist the reluctant support of Sir Rodolphe Forget, who had succeeded his father as president of the R&O and now faced a divided board. In 1913, Morden brought together the R&O with the Northern Navigation Company, the Inland Navigation Company and eight smaller firms (some of which had been absorbed earlier) to form Canada Steamship Lines. Before year's end, Morden had also added the Quebec Steamship Company, which operated to the West Indies and Bermuda, making CSL an ocean-going company as well — a legacy that would later be built on by Paul Martin.

The following years were a time of great turbulence for Canada Steamship Lines, and despite the bonanza that came with First World War contracts for shipping troops and grain across the Atlantic, its survival was by no means assured. The costs of refitting ships for the war effort and then refitting them again for civilian use, followed by a poorly conceived expansion and other strategic blunders on the part of top management, left CSL in 1922 under financial assault and unable to pay its bills. A group of New York financiers, recruited by the Montreal brokerage house Nesbitt, Thomson and Company (the same firm that spawned Power Corporation), rescued the company from imminent bankruptcy and installed William H. Coverdale, a Canadian citizen who divided his time between Canada and the United States, as president.

The Coverdale era spanned twenty-seven years, a time of financial stabilization despite the ravages of the Great Depression. His presidency was marked by a great expansion of both freight and passenger services, the redevelopment of the company's resort hotels, and diversification into areas that a debt-burdened Paul Martin would later get rid of: the acquisition of shipyards and the creation of a major trucking company, Kingsway Transport, from the amalgamation of several smaller firms. It was also under Coverdale that CSL carried out successful experiments with self-unloading bulk carriers, which in Martin's time would become the core of the company's business.

Coverdale's pride and joy was the elegant Great White Fleet of passenger vessels plying the Great Lakes, the St. Lawrence and the Saguenay, providing basic transport links for some customers but mostly carrying summer vacationers on short sightseeing trips or leisurely multi-day cruises. Some passengers stayed at the elaborate CSL-owned Manoir Richelieu resort hotel at Pointe-au-Pic, downriver from Quebec City, or at the simpler but still impressive Hotel Tadoussac, at the confluence of the St. Lawrence and the Saguenay. The West Indies and Bermuda services were long gone, sacrificed to pay the costs of a failed transatlantic foray by the previous management, but the Second World War turned CSL into a deep-sea carrier once again, shipping troops and supplies to Europe. Its shipyards, particularly its Davie Shipbuilding subsidiary at Lauzon near Quebec City, were pressed into service to help meet the requirements of the Canadian navy.

The immediate postwar era found Canada Steamship Lines in good shape but facing a whole new set of challenges. One was the continuing question of costs arising from the need to transship goods through the narrow canals that bypassed the rapids on the upper St. Lawrence between Montreal and Prescott, Ontario. Cargoes bound from the Great Lakes to Europe, for instance, had to be transferred at Kingston or Prescott to smaller, narrower vessels that could fit through the existing canals. (Some passenger vessels, with their lighter loads and shallower draughts, were designed to shoot the rapids.) This problem was resolved with the opening in 1959 of the St. Lawrence Seaway, which permitted the operation of vessels large enough to be operated economically over long distances.

But this created its own strains: almost overnight, CSL had to dispose of its uneconomic "canallers" and replace them with a whole new class of vessels designed to take maximum advantage of the greater dimensions of the new Seaway locks. This, of course, brought plenty of work to the CSL-owned shipyards on the Great Lakes and the St. Lawrence to fill orders both from CSL itself and from rival shipping companies. By the late 1960s, there were far fewer new orders, and the federal government was no longer offering the same level of protection and support to Canadian shipyards. One by one, the CSL yards at Fort William, Collingwood, Midland, Kingston and Lauzon were shut down or sold.

CSL's passenger vessels and hotels fared no better. Postwar generations of travellers seemed less interested in slow cruises and more attuned to the speed and convenience of the private automobile. In 1949 the CSL passenger ship on which the young Maurice Strong had once stowed away, the *Noronic*, was destroyed by a catastrophic fire while moored in Toronto harbour. One hundred and eighteen people lost their lives, most of them American tourists who had been sleeping in their berths awaiting an early morning departure.

Routes and vessels were dropped one by one. The Great Lakes routes were eliminated first. The St. Lawrence passenger service limped on until 1965, when the final three vessels were retired. The hotels, which had never been able to pay their own way with their short three-month season and had depended heavily on the ships to bring customers, were also disposed of.

In 1951, Sir James Dunn, the owner of Algoma Steel Company and various other business interests, acquired a controlling stake in Canada Steamship Lines. He had been buying stock gradually on the open market since 1939, when he recognized just how heavily his steel operations depended on shipping companies to bring ore to his mills, but it was not until he obtained the support of other major shareholders, notably J.W. McConnell, that he was able to cement his control. Dunn did not take an active role in management but insisted on deciding who would. He gave the nod to Rodgie McLagan, an engineer who ran the Canadian Vickers shipyard, chosen on the personal recommendation of the powerful and well-connected federal minister C.D. Howe. McLagan dominated CSL until his retirement, by stages, in the early 1960s.

Under McLagan's presidency CSL's profits rose and its debt declined. But among the less savoury aspects of this period was his cosy working relationship with Hal Banks, president of the Canadian branch of the U.S.-based Seafarers' International Union. The SIU had been brought into Canada in 1949, with the clear acquiescence of Ottawa, to oust the Communist-dominated Canadian Seamen's Union from its position as bargaining agent for workers at CSL and other inland shipping companies. Banks eventually became the subject of a federal probe into corruption and intimidation in the SIU. His lifestyle was more lavish than his salary could explain, his enemies suffered mysterious beatings, and union members lived under his tyranny. Banks maintained an effective blacklist, with the evident cooperation of the shipping companies, to keep his critics from finding work. He was a tough bargainer in wage talks, but was quick to sign contracts and remove strike threats without consulting the rank and file.

After McLagan pulled CSL out of the Lake Carriers' Association in 1956 during industry-wide labour talks, he established a closer relation with Banks than any of the other shipowners. Deals struck in private, often almost in secret, between Banks and McLagan became the norm in the industry — the first such deal was reached at the Westmount home of federal mediator H. Carl Goldenberg, whose son Eddie Goldenberg later became the trusted special assistant to Jean Chrétien. Other shipowners had little alternative but to fall into line behind CSL. As the years went by, Banks became increasingly aloof and abusive in his approach, drawing the growing ire of the broader Canadian labour movement and of many other Canadians as well. In the face of public pressure, Prime Minister John Diefenbaker appointed Mr. Justice Thomas Norris to head a special inquiry. The Norris report, issued in 1963, singled out CSL and McLagan for special criticism, saying they could have done much more to help maintain law and order on the Great Lakes. Banks was tried and convicted on a criminal charge but skipped bail and fled home to the U.S. Edgar Andrew Collard makes the following observations:

> Rodgie McLagan, as CSL's president, had replied to Judge Norris's accusations by charging Norris with unfairness ... [This defence] was unconvincing because

McLagan, in his relations with Banks, had gone beyond just making the worst of a bad situation. Hal Banks and CSL had reached agreements in contract after contract in a spirit of jovial friendship, bound happily together by mutual advantage ... [McLagan's] trouble was that his association with Banks had worked only too well. He and his company had profited too conspicuously from close dealings with a man denounced by Judge Norris as notorious.

Canada Steamship Lines: For Sale

Having put the Banks-McLagan era behind it, Canada Steamship Lines was brought into the orbit of Power Corporation, where it eventually came under the direction of Paul Martin. Martin described his attachment to the industries in which he was active with almost undisguised glee. "God, I love this business," he said in a 1984 interview with business writer David Olive. "I love the ships and buses and trucks. They're things you can touch, tangible things in a world full of numbers."

Numbers, though, have always played an important part in any business. The terms "downsizing" and "leveraged buyout" did not come into popular use until many years after Martin took the reins at CSL in 1973, but the concepts they embody have existed for a long time, and both were well known at Canada Steamship Lines. Downsizing can mean trimming staff or shutting entire divisions, as Martin had proved at Consolidated-Bathurst. Leveraged buyouts had been Paul Desmarais's specialty, and Martin took lessons from the master. At first Desmarais had employed LBOs in building his empire, but he later discovered their value in helping him dismember parts of it as well.

One example was furnished during the early years of Martin's presidency of CSL. Davie Shipbuilding was a continuing drain on the company, and Desmarais wanted out. At about this time, Louis Rochette, a former Davie executive who had gone over to rival Marine Industries at Sorel, decided that he wanted in. He and a group of three associates made an offer to buy Davie Shipbuilding from CSL with a small down payment and a large bank loan. They liked Davie's location and equipment, and they reasoned that their shallower pockets would make it easier to control wage costs. Desmarais was only too pleased to agree to their plans, and their success was not lost on Martin. (Rochette and his partners sold Davie in 1981 to Dome Petroleum, which was riding the crest of an oil boom and had been buying oil platforms from Davie. This attempt at vertical integration was not to last long. Dome was brought dramatically down to earth following a collapse in world oil prices, and Davie ended up as a ward of the Quebec government.)

The sale of Davie followed the disposal of three CSL-owned shipyards on the Great Lakes, leaving only the Collingwood yard still active in shipbuilding. It also followed the end of CSL's involvement in the passenger business and hotels. This was not called downsizing at the time, but CSL was shrinking its scope and would continue to do so. In the meantime, Paul Desmarais still had ambitious expansion plans for Power Corporation as a whole, and these plans would have a major impact on Paul Martin's career.

In the 1970s, Paul Desmarais became a byword for the upper reaches of Canadian business, both among his opponents and among his admirers. Power's homegrown character and francophone ownership did not prevent it from becoming a major target of the Quebec left: A 1971 strike at its flagship Montreal newspaper *La Presse* led to big demonstrations and a radicalization of Quebec's labour movement. A few years later Peter C. Newman devoted a long chapter to Desmarais in his book *The Canadian Establishment*. Indeed, Power Corporation attracted considerably more attention than another Montreal-based conglomerate, Canadian Pacific Limited, a venerable behemoth headquartered a few blocks away at historic Windsor Station (this was decades before a slimmed-down but still formidable Canadian Pacific decamped to Calgary). All the media ink devoted to Desmarais and Power Corporation, and the relative lack of attention paid to Canadian Pacific, belied the fact that CP was a far larger and mightier entity than Power.

What really rattled a few cages was Desmarais's announcement in April 1975 of an unsolicited bid to take over yet another conglomerate, Toronto-based Argus Corporation, then chaired by the elderly Bud McDougald, who shared control with two partners of the same generation. In the end, they decided not to sell, but meanwhile the idea of a combined Power-Argus entity sent shock waves across corporate and government circles, prompting Prime Minister Trudeau to appoint a Royal Commission of Inquiry into the Concentration of Corporate Power. The ensuing commission, chaired by veteran Ottawa mandarin Robert Bryce, produced little in the way of original thinking or recommendations, but the briefs it received and the witnesses it heard did provide some useful insights into the operations of big business in Canada.

The assets under Argus's control included Massey-Ferguson (then a world leader in farm equipment), paper-maker Domtar, Dominion Stores (a big but declining supermarket chain), Hollinger Mines and Standard Broadcasting. Desmarais and McDougald both appeared as witnesses before the Bryce Commission, and the differences in their respective approaches to corporate control were instructive. Desmarais said he preferred to have 100 per cent ownership of companies under his control because minority shareholders could be a nuisance. McDougald, on the other hand, said a holding of as little as 15 per cent was adequate to assure control if it enabled his appointees to dominate the executive committee. Argus's relatively small asset levels indeed made it an easier takeover target, since financing needs would be less onerous. A few years later Conrad Black, by then dealing with the widows of McDougald and his partners, charmed them into selling out. Some of the holdings had seen better days. Under Black's stewardship, Massey-Ferguson forsook tractors for auto parts, changed its name to Varity, and moved its head office to the United States. Varity and most other parts of the former Argus empire were sold off. Hollinger Mines abandoned the mining business and became simply Hollinger Inc., the main holding company for Black's extensive newspaper holdings, which grew to include Southam Inc.

Desmarais's most ambitious target, which he also failed to snag, was the colossus itself, Canadian Pacific. Through the late 1970s and into the early 1980s, he gradually built a sizeable holding in CP shares, passing the 10 per cent mark that can often trigger alarm bells. Had he been offered other large blocks of CP shares and won the active support of the Caisse de Dépôt et Placement du Québec, the province's public pension fund administrator which itself held close to 10 per cent of Canadian Pacific, he might have been able to mount a credible run for control.

In launching an assault on Canadian Pacific, Desmarais needed to raise a stronger cash position to support his bid. It was in this context that he put Canada Steamship Lines up for sale in June 1981. The need for additional cash was not the only reason for Desmarais's decision. He also feared regulatory problems if he succeeded in his ambition of taking over Canadian Pacific, since the inland shipping and railway industries compete for certain types of cargo. In addition, Martin was asking for money to buy new vessels, and Power Corporation, whose accounts were consolidated with those of CSL, was unwilling to provide the funds. Finally, changing conditions in the shipping industry meant that CSL was going to require management resources that Desmarais was not willing to commit.

Desmarais asked Martin to find a suitable buyer. Martin replied that he would like to buy CSL himself. One potentially insurmountable obstacle Martin faced was that he possessed no great personal wealth and did not have the money to pay for the purchase. This meant he would have to find a partner. It also meant that he would have to borrow heavily. In other words, this was going to be a leveraged buyout. Desmarais was in a hurry, and Martin had little time to lose in lining up partners or financing. If he failed, he would still have to find another buyer for CSL. Martin went to visit Laurence Pathy, a longstanding friend and scion of a Montreal family with a long involvement in the shipping industry. Pathy was president of Fednav Limited, whose main operating subsidiary was Federal Commerce and Navigation Limited, a large — for a time the largest — Canadian-owned ocean shipping company. According to published accounts, Pathy agreed almost immediately to join Martin as an equal partner in the takeover of Canada Steamship Lines. Martin threw in what modest assets he could — putting on the line "virtually every cent I had and could scare up," he told David Olive — but obtained the great bulk of the required funds from the Royal Bank, which on numerous occasions had also helped meet Desmarais's financial needs. The sale price was $195 million, which was about $50 million more than Power had paid for CSL in a buyout that had begun eighteen years earlier and was spread over twelve years.

Laurence Pathy, whom Martin chose as his partner in the buyout of CSL, is one of the wealthiest and most powerful people in Canadian shipping. He has managed nonetheless to maintain a low personal profile even by the standards of an industry noted for its secretive nature. Pathy, born in 1934, is said to have granted only one interview to a journalist in his entire career, and that was with the editor of a trade publication who has covered the Montreal shipping scene for decades. Pathy declines even to permit an entry in the *Canadian Who's Who*. His listing in the 1998 *Financial Post Directory of Directors* shows him only as president and chief executive officer of Fednav Ltd., not indicating any involvement in other companies or in any charitable or nonprofit groups.

Most shipping companies in Canada, including CSL and Fednav, refrain from listing their shares on the stock exchange, which means their financial statements do not have to be made public. In certain other instances, most notably Canadian Pacific's hefty shipping division (which has grown enormously through acquisitions in recent years), the finances of shipping operations are consolidated with those of a publicly traded parent company and are not broken out separately. Some shipping companies seem reluctant even to reveal basic information such as how many vessels they have in their fleets, although such information is usually well known to their rivals. Shipowners are a very clubby group, however, meeting regularly through their trade associations and at myriad social gatherings. There are far fewer secrets among them than there are between individual companies and the general public. Fednav operates more than seventy vessels, mostly under charter, and has annual revenues in excess of $700 million, ranking it among the biggest privately held and independently owned companies in Canada.

The entity formed by Martin and Pathy to buy out CSL was called The CSL Group Inc. and became the parent company of Canada Steamship Lines. In forming a partnership with Passage Holdings Inc., Martin's personal holding company, Fednav put up $35 million in preferred shares and agreed to finance three new ships that were either under construction or planned for imminent construction.

Despite the additional cash he obtained by selling CSL, Paul Desmarais fell short in his drive to take over Canadian Pacific. Ugly rumours at the time, never credibly quashed, suggested that certain major CP shareholders were displeased by the prospect of a French Canadian taking control and made it clear their shares were not for sale. For whatever reason, Desmarais abandoned his quest for Canadian Pacific and turned his attention instead to acquisitions in European financial corporations, dismantling much of his Canadian empire in the course of the 1980s. Montreal Trust was sold to Bell Canada Enterprises (which later sold it to the Bank of Nova Scotia), while Consolidated-Bathurst was acquired by Chicago-based Stone Container (later returning to Canadian control in a merger with Abitibi-Price to form Abitibi Consolidated). Power Corporation, no longer the stuff of royal commissions, became a might-have-been.

Shipping Magnate

The company that Paul Martin took over was caught in one of its many periods of transition. The high debt level carried by CSL under its new ownership was made more onerous by sharp rises in interest rates. The Steel Company of Canada, a major customer, was shut by a strike at the moment of the purchase. Voyageur Enterprises, CSL's bus subsidiary, was also shut by a strike. These problems were mere symptoms of what was to come.

Shifts in Canada's trading patterns meant that more freight was moving across the Pacific and a smaller proportion was moving through the Great Lakes and the St. Lawrence. A new program of federal subsidies to grain farmers for railway ship-ments through the Rockies, introduced in 1984 and aimed at maintaining the age-old Crow Rate, diverted some business that might otherwise have gone through the Lakes. This com-pounded problems faced by shipowners in the eastern half of the country. The North American steel industry, a major client of these shipowners with its heavy requirements for iron ore and coal, was shrinking in the face of competition from lower-cost overseas producers. Other traditional industries were con-fronting similar dislocation. CSL's remaining shipyards were afflicted by excess capacity. The Kingsway trucking subsidi-ary, beset by intense competition and strong fluctuations in demand, also faced an uncertain future. Raymond Lemay, who headed CSL's shipping operations in 1986, remarked that more than thirty cargo vessels of the 110 that CSL and other com-panies placed in service on the Canadian side of the Lakes had been laid up, and this was in the midst of a North American economic boom.

The combination of grain and iron ore had been lucrative for CSL. Bulk carriers would leave the Great Lakes laden with grain and transfer their cargoes to ocean-going vessels at the port of Sept-Îles, on the north shore of the Gulf of St. Lawrence, returning to the Lakes with full cargoes of iron ore from the mines of Labrador and contiguous parts of Quebec, brought to the coast by railway. Vessels that generate revenues on both their outbound and inbound legs spell profits for their owners; if they lose this backhaul revenue, they can become unprofitable. Sharp production declines in the U.S. steel industry in the early 1980s, and lesser declines in the more modern Canadian steel industry, coincided with a revival of mining in Minnesota's Mesabi range thanks to new metallurgical procedures that made certain low-grade ores more valuable. The effects of the resulting drop in demand for Labrador and Quebec ore included a decision, carried out by Brian Mulroney in his role as president of the Iron Ore Company of Canada, to shut virtually the entire town of Schefferville with the closing of the local mines. They also included a partial loss of CSL's important backhaul business.

CSL and other shipping companies faced additional difficulties, some of them imposed by government. Ships passing through Canada's inland waters were required to use the services of local pilotage authorities, often at exorbitant cost, even when the captains were Canadians who had an initimate knowledge of these waterways. As well, a steady rise in tolls on the St. Lawrence Seaway, intended to reflect true costs more accurately, drove business away and created a vicious cycle, with tolls having to rise further to make up for the lost business.

A team assembled by Paul Martin set out to generate new business by taking advantage of CSL's traditional expertise in the design and operation of self-unloading bulk carriers. This was wedded to Martin's personal conviction about the importance of international trade to Canada's future and his resulting desire to return CSL to the role it had filled on earlier brief occasions as a deep-sea carrier. It is almost axiomatic that increased trade favours those involved in the shipment of goods. The further the goods have to travel, the greater the revenues that accrue to the owners of the ships and other conveyances that carry them. Both then and now, however, the great bulk of the commodities and manufactured goods produced by Canadians have been sent to points within North America. As foreign trade grows in importance to the Canadian economy, with about 40 per cent of all production exported as the twentieth century draws to a close, a rising proportion of these exports, more than 80 per cent, are sold to buyers in the United States. Simple arithmetic shows that less than 8 per cent of what Canadians produce finds buyers in countries other than Canada and the U.S.

Through most of its existence, CSL has been both a beneficiary and a prisoner of this situation. Because most Canadian cargo traffic moves within North America, this is where the business has been generated, and this is where CSL has earned its revenues. Martin set out to modify this orientation, though by no means to reverse it. Under his ownership and management, CSL continued to emphasize its traditional role on the Great Lakes and the St. Lawrence, but to this it added a modest deep-sea fleet, fulfilling his dreams of being a true international trader. The extensive investment and management effort required to bring about this partial transformation of CSL may have been one of the reasons Paul Desmarais became interested in selling the company. Desmarais generally took on the role of passive investor, with little interest in overseeing radical changes in the companies under his control. According to a close associate, Martin had been advocating the acquisition of a deep-sea fleet even before the opportunity arose for him to take over CSL.

Martin's move into ocean shipping helped precipitate the end of his partnership with Laurence Pathy in 1988. Fednav and CSL had been seen as complementary in many ways. Despite its 50 per cent equity holding in CSL, Fednav kept its operations separate from those of CSL, which remained under the management control of Paul Martin. At some point Martin and Pathy experienced what appears to have been an amicable parting. Martin's continuing push into ocean shipping, although on a small scale, made CSL more of a rival to Fednav than it had been when the original deal was struck. There was also unconfirmed gossip in shipping circles suggesting that Pathy was not entirely happy with the quality of management at CSL. For whatever reasons, the partnership was dissolved. The CSL Group Inc. announced that it had purchased Fednav's 50 per cent holding, effective March 31, 1988, leaving Passage Holdings, Martin's company, in possession of all common shares. At the same time, Martin announced the creation of a wholly owned subsidiary, CSL Equity Investments Limited, that would hold all CSL assets outside the core business of bulk shipping. He also proclaimed his determination to continue building CSL's business to Europe and the U.S. east coast while maintaining the Great Lakes as the prime focus.

One of CSL's continuing strengths has been its pioneering work in the development and refinement of self-unloading bulk carriers. In past eras, ships carrying grain, coal, mineral ores or other bulk commodities would have to be unloaded using mechanical shovels, scoop by scoop. This process, still in widespread use today in many parts of the world, is slow and laborious. Self-unloading carriers rely on gravity and on systems of belts and pulleys. Bulk cargoes in the holds of ships fall onto moving belts, which carry them above the deck and load them directly into storage silos, railway hopper cars or other ships. Besides being faster and requiring less labour, this system is especially useful at ports with limited onshore facilities, since the ship itself carries most of the equipment required for unloading cargoes. Although CSL did not invent the self-unloader, it has used this technology extensively since the 1920s and has become recognized worldwide as a leader in its application. Recent refinements developed by CSL include articulated unloading arms and covers to prevent dust contamination.

Once Martin took control of CSL in 1981, he appointed a marketing team headed by comptroller Fred Pitre, later named executive vice-president. This team did more than its predecessors to consolidate shipments bound for different customers, making more efficient use of vessels. It also succeeded in taking some business from the railways — for instance, using self-unloaders to carry Saskatchewan potash from the Lakehead to U.S. ports. The ship-to-ship capabilities of self-unloaders also made it easier to transfer cargoes from narrow vessels designed to fit the St. Lawrence Seaway locks to the largest ocean-going vessels at ports such as Sept-Îles; this capability led to a big increase in coal shipments.

CSL's self-unloaders also began to carry overseas cargoes from U.S. east coast ports such as Baltimore and Norfolk that were too shallow for the deepest-draught vessels, transferring them to bigger ships in Nova Scotia's Strait of Canso for onward shipment. CSL also moved self-unloaders to ocean service. Its first overseas customer was Portline, a Lisbon-based shipping line serving a coal-fired electricity plant in southern Portugal situated near the coast but far from suitable port facilities; self-unloaders reduced delivery costs of coal significantly. CSL self-unloaders even developed an intra-European business, carrying ores from giant vessels at Rotterdam to smaller European ports. After Martin withdrew from active management of the company, CSL sold most of its conventional bulk carriers on the Great Lakes to concentrate mostly on self-unloaders, and began to assess the possibility of operating self-unloaders in Southeast Asia.

A Cautious Steward

At the same time as it developed its overseas business, CSL was becoming a less Canadian carrier in some important respects. To avoid high Canadian wage costs, some vessels were reflagged and staffed with foreign crews. (Later this attracted obvious barbs in the House of Commons from Bloc Québéois leader Gilles Duceppe.) CSL also found itself turning to foreign shipyards for the construction of most of its vessels, including an initial order with the Verolme shipyard in Brazil for six vessels, the first of which entered service in 1988.

Martin was president of CSL, though not its owner, when Davie Shipbuilding was sold. When he took over CSL from Power Corporation in 1981, CSL still had one active shipbuilding yard, located at Collingwood, on Ontario's Georgian Bay. Collingwood was the headquarters of CSL's Canadian Shipbuilding and Engineering subsidiary. Its Midland and Kingston yards had been closed in 1955 and 1965, respectively, while the Port Arthur yard at Thunder Bay was kept open only to perform maintenance work. Jim Elder (later to become CSL president), the naval architect brought in to run the Collingwood yard, showed great ingenuity in improving production methods and ship designs, but a dearth of orders and capriciously applied federal government support for shipyards led to a decision in 1985 to close the yard. Following a series of negotiations, the yard was closed in 1986, with a generous severance package for the remaining workers. Meanwhile, CSL became 50 per cent owner of a new joint venture with ULS International, owner of the Port Weller drydocks at St. Catharines. CSL's Port Arthur operations were folded into this new company.

Martin's slimming down of CSL did not end there. The trucking industry was undergoing a new wave of consolidation. Management at Kingsway Transport, the trucking subsidiary, determined that the company either had to grow by acquiring other trucking lines or see its relative position weakened as its rivals acquired other companies. With CSL striving to finance the construction of self-unloading ocean ships, and with Martin still battling to pay down the debt from his 1981 leveraged buyout, funds simply were not available to expand the trucking operations. In a deal that took effect in 1987, Don Freeman, a Toronto freight forwarder, took control of Kingsway in yet another LBO. Like Desmarais, Martin had learned the secret of using leveraged buyouts both to acquire and to dispose of assets.

The Voyageur bus line presented problems all its own. It faced declines in ridership resulting partly from the subsidized competition provided by Via Rail passenger trains but more significantly from rising rates of car travel. During the Desmarais years, Voyageur acquired a number of smaller lines and brought most remaining feeder lines into an affiliated network. It came to blanket most populated areas of Quebec and eastern Ontario. Under Martin, starting shortly before he left CSL management to enter politics, this course was sharply reversed. Nearly all of Voyageur's routes were sold, piecemeal, to other companies, often with non-union workforces. The biggest single chunk of the operation, covering routes linking Montreal with Quebec City and points east, was sold to a group of former Voyageur managers, who named their new company Orléans Express. Once the biggest Canadian-owned intercity bus line, Voyageur nearly ceased to exist. By 1998 its only major route was between Montreal and Ottawa.

When he stood in the 1988 parliamentary election in LaSalle–Émard riding, Paul Martin had been president of Canada Steamship Lines for fifteen years and an owner for seven. Under his ownership, the company had carved itself a new niche with its ocean-going self-unloaders but had shed most of its interests outside its core shipping business. Martin's assiduous efforts to pay down the company's debt had had the effect of considerably enhancing the value of his own equity position in CSL. By the late 1980s he was the possessor of a sizeable personal fortune, although since most of it consisted of his interest in a privately held company its exact worth was difficult to calculate (in a 1989 newspaper account it was estimated at between $10 and $20 million). Other assets included his Westmount house and his farm in the Eastern Townships. Sometimes characterized as a "country estate," this property is described by a close friend of Martin's as "just a bloody old farm. There's a house on the property, and he has somebody who works the farm for him."

When Martin was elected to the House of Commons, he retained his ownership of CSL but gave up his active management role in the company. On December 8, 1988, he turned over the presidency to Jim Elder, former head of the Colling-wood shipyard and, more recently, executive vice-president of CSL. He made a number of other executive appointments that same day, leaving behind a management structure that would have to be swept aside several years later. At about the same time, he gave up his directorships on the boards of Fednav Ltd., the reconstituted Canadian Shipbuilding and Engineering, Imasco Corp. (parent comany of Imperial Tobacco, Canada's leading nicotine supplier), Manufacturers Life Insurance, Red-path Industries (a sugar refiner), and CB Pak (the packaging unit of Consolidated-Bathurst).

This did not mean, of course, that all ties other than owner-ship were cut between Martin and CSL. He continued to review financial statements, and he began drawing a pension from CSL, although in keeping with his previous policy, he declined to pay himself any dividends. All profits went towards meeting the company's investment requirements and paying down the debt resulting from the original leveraged buyout in 1981. This debt had ballooned considerably with the purchase early in 1988 of Fednav's 50 per cent share in CSL, and interest pay-ments would become especially onerous with the tight-money policies that Bank of Canada governor John Crow was about to implement. This helped make Martin acutely aware of how quickly compound interest can make debt levels swell, and it probably contributed to the anti-deficit zeal he would later display as finance minister. By 1998, however, the company's debt had been largely eliminated.

Canada's long recession of the early 1990s, induced at least in part by the high interest rates wielded by Ottawa to ratchet down inflation, again found Canada Steamship Lines in diffi-culty. Martin, then sitting as an opposition member of the House of Commons, asked Tony Chesterman, an old friend and former neighbour, to take over as CSL chair and chief execu-tive officer. Chesterman's background was in advertising. His main connection to the shipping industry had consisted of contracts to manage advertising and public relations for CSL.

The approach he took in his new job mirrored in part that taken by William Coverdale in 1922: He sold off some vessels, sought new ways to reduce expenses, and reorganized the vertical executive structure then in place, eliminating costly layers of middle management and promoting more effective cooperation between divisions with a more horizontal style of management and the appointment of new division heads. Chesterman's two-year remake of the company concluded in 1993. He stayed on as chief executive officer for a further two years before going into semi-retirement.

Martin did not commit any obvious blunders at CSL, but neither can his time as CSL president be characterized as particularly dynamic. He showed great courage in buying out the company in 1981, in partnership with Fednav, but in retrospect his stewardship seems distinctly cautious. When he took over, shipping operations accounted for about half CSL's revenues, with the rest coming from highway operations, split almost evenly between Kingsway trucks and Voyageur buses. By the end of the decade, Kingsway was gone and Voyageur was almost gone. There were sound reasons for both moves, not least a need to pay down debt, but they were not balanced by anything more than modest growth on the shipping side.

This approach is not hard to explain. Conditions for the inland shipping industry were difficult in the early 1980s, especially with the sharp contraction in revenues from the steel industry. Martin countered by moving into ocean shipping, where potential revenues were greater and where some of his dreams lay. But again, this move was undertaken with caution. In effect, CSL was becoming a niche operator, specializing in self-unloading bulk carriers, not just in its limited deep-sea services but increasingly in its traditional Great Lakes stronghold. CSL had the technology and the experience to compete effectively in this part of the business, and Martin was not about to risk the company in what, for CSL, would have been a more difficult and dangerous competitive strategy.

This guarded stance probably had much to do with CSL's financial structure. When a company is highly leveraged, with its nominal owners holding only a limited amount of equity, even a minor downturn can wreak havoc with the balance sheet. To avoid the risk of being wiped out, anyone without a reckless gambler's instinct would have pursued a careful approach. And Paul Martin has shown that he is not a reckless gambler.

CHAPTER THREE

The Road to Political Power

Whated as leader of the Liberal Party in 1984, one of the names that circulated briefly as a possible candidate to succeed him was that of Paul Martin, Jr. "It's logical that Paul is considered leadership material," said Maurice Strong. "He's a fresh face in a party that has drawn its last four prime ministers from outside the immediate circle of obvious contenders." But the Liberals quickly settled on another "outsider," John Turner, whose association with the Trudeau government had been effaced by nine years of practising corporate law in Toronto. Turner won the leadership at the Liberals' June convention and led them into a disastrous election in which they won only forty seats. As soon as the dust settled from this calamity, Turner's leadership was put in question, and his resignation or ouster was a constant possibility. In these circumstances there was renewed speculation about the succession, and this time — especially after Jean Chrétien resigned from Parliament in 1986 — Paul Martin's name was at or near the top of the list.

Martin had significant assets that made up for his virtually complete lack of political experience. There was the famous Liberal name. There was his success as head of a major corporation. There was his association with the ever-influential Power Corporation nexus. He had long been active as a Liberal fundraiser and organizer, and had made a positive impression when he had chaired candidates' debates during the 1984 leadership campaign. He was neither identified with the shambles of the Turner regime nor seen as a leader-in-exile like Chrétien. Moreover, as Strong pointed out, his status as a political novice could itself be turned into an asset. Reporter Susan Riley noted that the 1980s were conducive to

> a strange, little-analysed development in mainstream political parties. They no longer choose their leaders at noisy conventions, where people wear silly hats and drink too much, although they still hold such conventions. The conventions merely anoint leaders discovered earlier by trolling through corporate boardrooms. Ordinary MPs are no longer good enough.

Both Turner and the politician he faced across the floor in the House of Commons, Prime Minister Brian Mulroney, had come to the leadership of their respective parties from outside politics, although both had considerably more political experience than Martin.

While severe misgivings about Turner's leadership lingered and schemes to replace him persisted throughout the Tories' first term and even into the 1988 election campaign, the Martin leadership scenario never quite materialized. Turner survived his most serious challenge, the leadership review at the Liberals' annual convention in November 1986. And as attention swung from Tory cabinet minister John Fraser and tainted tuna to the dubious wheeling and dealing of Sinclair Stevens to André Bissonnette's misadventures with Oerlikon Aerospace, the growing unpopularity of the Mulroney government kept the Liberals consistently at or near the top of the polls.

Star Candidate

Martin's leadership plans were not abandoned, only deferred. He would run for Parliament, and as a "star candidate," in the next election. Martin lived in Westmount, and that safely Liberal constituency was open after MP Donald Johnston resigned from John Turner's caucus in January 1988. However, Martin had already decided to run in the much less opulent riding of LaSalle–Émard, consisting of the Montreal neighbourhood of Ville Émard and the suburb of Ville LaSalle in the southwest corner of Montreal Island. Historically Liberal, LaSalle–Émard had fallen to the Tories in their 1984 sweep. Its sitting member was Claude Lanthier, a consulting engineer with deep roots in the riding.

Montreal bus route number 36 has its eastern terminus at the edge of Old Montreal next to the tall, austere Stock Exchange Tower, just half a block from the smaller, more ornate Canada Steamship Lines building, which also houses the headquarters of Power Corporation of Canada. This was the place where on most days Paul Martin went to the office. The bus passes the backside of stately old Windsor Station as it winds its way along the desolate southwestern fringe of downtown Montreal, then meanders through the neighbourhoods of Little Burgundy, Saint-Henri and Côte-Saint-Paul — a combination of working-class monotony, urban decay and recent gentrification. At the western end of Côte-Saint-Paul the bus turns south, crossing the Lachine Canal into Ville Émard.

Ville Émard was once a self-contained village. In 1910 it was formally annexed by the City of Montreal, although it retains its pre-annexation moniker even today. The number 36 bus runs the entire length of Monk Boulevard, a simple thoroughfare connecting street upon street of typical prewar Montreal housing, characterized by tightly knit rows of duplexes and triplexes, providing high density, with each dwelling having its own entrance from the street. There are many small businesses along Monk Boulevard, and the area gives a general impression of modest comfort and modest ambition. This part of town is mostly residential and largely French-speaking. The bus makes a few twists and turns, past newer streets dotted with simple bungalows and small apartment buildings, before finally reaching the Angrignon Métro station, adjacent to the sprawling city park of the same name.

The Angrignon station is a major transfer point, with several bus routes radiating westward into Ville LaSalle. The number 110 runs through street after street of semi-detached duplexes, built in the postwar era as Ville LaSalle grew from a sleepy village of 3,000 people to an industrial town of 75,000, and then along LaSalle Boulevard, the town's waterfront drive and the site of most of its history. It passes a small park where the parish church stood when the area was the fief of Robert Cavelier, Sieur de La Salle, the explorer, dreamer and con artist who helped extend France's North American empire to the Gulf of Mexico in the seventeenth century. A little farther west is a windmill built by a Scottish entrepreneur named William Fleming in the early nineteenth century — one of only twenty remaining windmills in Quebec. Before leaving Ville LaSalle the number 110 passes the municipality's imposing city hall, a converted Burroughs-Wellcome pharmaceutical factory built in 1930 near the western end of the Lachine Canal. Heading back towards Angrignon on the number 113, the rider travels through busy commercial streets and past a large Seagram's distillery, one of Ville LaSalle's leading employers (Labatt, Monsanto and Siemens are other major corporations with plants in the area), as well as many smaller factories.

As of 1988 LaSalle–Émard was more than half francophone, but it also had substantial anglophone and immigrant populations. An ambitious bilingual politician who wanted to demonstrate a common touch could hardly find a better place to land. Showing his commitment to the riding, Martin even endeavoured to take a condominium in Ville Émard, although he never actually lived there. After Paul was elected, the Martins lived primarily in Ottawa. They sold their opulent Westmount home — now too large for the family since their three sons had grown up and moved out — and switched their Montreal base to a townhouse on Simpson Street in the elite northwest corner of the city's downtown, the Square Mile.

On May 29, 1988, in the presence of his father, Paul Martin was officially nominated as Liberal candidate in LaSalle–Émard. With no one else seeking the nomination, the only dissenting note was provided by striking employees of CSL-owned Voyageur bus lines, who stood outside the hall and booed Martin as he arrived. In his acceptance speech, Martin criticized the Tory government's free trade deal with the United States, initialled in late 1987: "If this free trade agreement stands, any possibility of Canada developing a modern industrial policy will have gone out the window."

On one level, there was nothing surprising about Martin's criticism of the free trade deal. The Liberals had distinguished themselves from the Tories by opposing the deal, and Martin was simply following the party line. On the other hand, the business community of which Martin was so much a part was solidly behind free trade — especially in Quebec. At the very outset of his political career, Martin was already confronted with the task of managing the delicate interface between business and politics, which would occupy much of his attention and energy in the years to come.

By no stretch of the imagination could Paul Martin be described as ever having been anti-business, but he did come to politics with somewhat different ideas about the relationship between business and government from those prevailing in Tory Ottawa. In fact, one characteristic that has made Martin unusual in both business and political circles is not so much the particular ideas he has held but that he is open to and interested in a variety of ideas in the first place. He always maintained that he entered politics not to seek the Liberal leadership but to advance his ideas, and there is no doubt some truth to that assertion.

The Mulroney government, while not as fixedly ideological as Ronald Reagan's administration in Washington or Margaret Thatcher's in London, accepted the free-market nostrums of the day. The government's economic blueprint, tabled in the House of Commons by Finance Minister Michael Wilson barely two months after the Tories came to power in 1984, condemned "expansive, intrusive government" and promised "a revitalization of the private sector as the driving force behind growth and job creation." The chief expression of the Conservative approach was the free trade deal, which placed limits on a variety of forms of government action.

Martin was more impressed with the kind of business–government cooperation that in the 1980s was proving so successful in Japan, as well as with the modified version of this model being experimented with in Quebec. By the late 1980s, with the help and encouragement of Quebec government institutions such as Quebec Stock Savings Plans and the Caisse de Dépôt et Placement (and of the federal government as well), an indigenous Quebec business class had developed substantially. Martin had close associations with this group even if he was not fully part of it, and he believed that the policies that had helped develop it could be extended to the rest of Canada. He told Carol Goar of the Toronto *Star* in a 1989 interview,

> What Quebec has created in the last twenty-five years is nothing less than an economic revolution. It has gone from being everyone else's doormat — a sterile, inward-looking economy — to being one of the most dynamic economies in North America. Canada is desperately in need of the same kind of revolution.

Martin attributed the "revolution" to three factors: an internal self-help network among Quebec entrepreneurs, a huge pool of capital made available to promising businesses through the Caisse de Dépôt, and business–government cooperation:

> Nobody believes in a strict demarcation between the public and private sectors any more. Quebec got where it is today by a more sophisticated degree of cooperation between the government and the private sector than has ever been seen in Canada.

Thus, while Martin was not opposed to free trade as such, he did believe in at least some forms of government intervention and he saw the free trade agreement as precluding them.

Braving the Tory Tide

Had the system operated in its usual fashion, Parliament could have ratified the free trade agreement and Mulroney could have gone into the approaching election with the deal as a *fait accompli*, the crowning achievement of his first term. John Turner ensured that the system did not operate in its usual fashion by instructing the Liberal majority in the Senate not to pass the free trade deal unless it received a popular mandate in an election. Turner's Senate gambit turned the election into a quasi-referendum on free trade, and also limited Mulroney's options in terms of timing. In early October 1988 Mulroney dissolved Parliament and called an election for November 21.

In LaSalle–Émard, Paul Martin had no assurance of a successful launch to his political career. Claude Lanthier had won the seat for the Tories by about 4,000 votes in 1984, and he was an assiduous constituency MP. Furthermore, the Tories had moved back into the lead in the polls, and the Liberals still faced serious financial and organizational problems. Reports of Liberal division and disarray, including a rather flimsy rumour that some Liberals would ask Turner to resign in mid-campaign, persisted through much of October.

Nowhere were the Liberals' problems more serious than in Quebec. After dominating federal politics in Quebec for most of the twentieth century, the Liberals had managed to win only seventeen of its seventy-five seats in 1984, and it appeared that they would be doing well to hang on to that many in 1988. The party was deeply divided between Turner loyalists and Trudeau Liberals who would have been happier with Jean Chrétien as leader. Nor was it just a question of personalities. The Trudeau Liberals were unhappy with Turner's support of the Meech Lake constitutional accord, which if ratified would secure Quebec's signature on the constitution (withheld at the time of repatriation in 1982) in exchange for recognition of Quebec as a "distinct society" and other provisions. In addition, Turner's opposition to free trade had alienated the party from the Quebec Liberals, who under Premier Robert Bourassa were a powerful force. Prominent Liberals decided to sit the election out, and unseemly nomination squabbles attracted unwanted attention. Polls showed the Liberals running third, swamped by the Tories and even behind the NDP, which had never taken a seat in Quebec.

The campaign in LaSalle–Émard revolved primarily around local issues — plant closings, pollution in the Lachine Canal, daycare spaces (which Martin promised to double) — and personalities, and Martin escaped some of the worst effects of the disaster unfolding around him. He was loyal to Turner's position on Meech Lake — a stance that, along with his business credentials, made him one of the few Liberal candidates to earn an endorsement from Premier Bourassa. Nevertheless, three weeks into the campaign senior Liberals were saying that the roughly half a dozen safe Liberal seats in Quebec did not include LaSalle–Émard.

In the country as a whole, the prospect of a Tory cakewalk and a Liberal fiasco masked a deeper political unease. The focus of this unease was the free trade agreement. Especially in English Canada, the deal raised fears of a loss of Canadian identity in a homogeneous North America. At the same time, people feared being left behind in a fast-moving, competitive, globalized world if the deal were not signed. There was also a widespread sense that despite (or perhaps because of) the Mulroney government's attempts to "sell" the deal, it had not been adequately explained. Was the agreement just a trade deal, as the Tories maintained, or would it affect Canada's entire economic and political future, as its opponents argued? Depending on how one read the deal, everything from Canadian culture to health care and social programs to water diversion could be affected by its passage, which made it possible for opponents to argue — as did Paul Martin — that they were not against free trade as such but rather against the provisions of this particular agreement.

Even if the deal was consciously or subconsciously on people's minds, the only politician who wanted to talk about it in the early weeks of the campaign was John Turner, and he was going nowhere. The Tories insisted that the most important election issue was not free trade but "managing change," while the NDP was more intent on attacking Turner's credibility as an opponent of free trade than the deal itself.

That all changed during the English-language television debate on October 25, when the Liberal leader's aggressive pursuit of Mulroney on free trade and the prime minister's weak response finally persuaded the electorate to take Turner's crusade seriously. All along he had insisted that the agreement was more than just a trade deal that was, in Mulroney's description, "cancellable on six months' notice." Now Turner effectively made opposition to free trade a matter of patriotism:

> We built a country east and west and north. We built it on an infrastructure that deliberately resisted the continental pressure of the United States. For one hundred and twenty years, we have done it. With one signature of a pen, you have reversed that, thrown us into the north-south influence of the United States, and will reduce us, I am sure, to a colony of the United States, because when the economic levers go, the political independence is sure to follow.

In the history of the Liberal Party, the 1988 election campaign stands as a unique event. The Liberals had spent decades governing largely on behalf of corporate Canada and in the postwar era had presided over Canada's integration into the American economy. In 1984, they had chosen John Turner as their leader in the hope that he could repair the party's ties with the corporate sector, which had become somewhat frayed in the Trudeau era. Four years later, this same party under this same leader was conducting a crusade against a further step in continental integration that had almost unanimous corporate backing. In the 1988 election, only one party had the enthusiastic support of the corporate sector: the Conservatives.

But things were a little different in LaSalle–Émard, where corporate donations accounted for slightly over half the roughly $90,000 raised by Paul Martin's campaign. The shipping sector was a significant source of funds, with Canadian Shipbuilding and Engineering contributing $5,000, Fednav supplying $4,000 and Matt Shipyard kicking in $3,000. Other corporate donors included Polysar ($7,500), Maclean Hunter ($3,000), Redpath Industries ($2,500) and Oerlikon Aerospace ($2,000). Martin's corporate colleagues were also well represented among individual contributors, among them Lorne Webster of the Prenor holding company and the prominent Westmount family ($4,150), Canadian Pacific chief executive officer William Stinson ($500) and Bronfman business adviser Senator Leo Kolber ($500).

John Turner's argument that the free trade agreement threatened the future of Canada struck a deep chord outside Quebec. Immediately after the debate, poll results showed a surge in Liberal strength, throwing the election into doubt. In the last few weeks of the campaign, the Tories succeeded in stanching the flow with their own attack on Turner's credibility. Business did its part by stepping up its campaign in favour of free trade, threatening what amounted to an investment strike if the deal was not passed. International speculators put severe downward pressure on the Canadian dollar as the Liberals' poll numbers rose. And yet on election day the Tories managed to salvage only 48 per cent of the seats in English Canada — down from 74 per cent in 1984 and even marginally lower than 1980, when the Liberals had won a majority.

However, as frequently happens in federal elections, the campaign in Quebec took its own path. While there was opposition to free trade in Quebec, it focused on the economic effects of the deal, and Turner's pro-Canada crusade had little resonance. Premier Bourassa and Quebec business leaders campaigned heavily for the deal. The star recruit into Mulroney's cabinet, Lucien Bouchard, posed free trade as a Quebec-versus-Ontario issue. In contrast to the results in the rest of the country, the Tories scored a net gain of five seats in Quebec, reducing the Liberals' Quebec caucus to a historic low of twelve members. One of the twelve was Paul Martin. The race in LaSalle–Émard remained tight until the end, and Mulroney campaigned in the riding with only days to go until the election, telling party supporters that "the Liberals have become Canada's Luddites." Nevertheless, Martin won his hard-fought battle with Claude Lanthier by a little over a thousand votes, with the margin of victory largely being obtained in anglophone and allophone areas of Ville LaSalle. LaSalle–Émard was one of only two Quebec seats that switched from the Tories to the Liberals.

A Ticking Time Bomb

It is no small irony that the most prominent business Liberal of the 1990s got his political start in an election in which the business community and the Liberal Party found themselves on opposite sides of one of the most intense issues in recent Canadian political history. The overall Tory majority ensured that the free trade agreement would now be ratified, and the Liberals had to decide how they would adjust to the new reality. Less than a month after the election, the government called Parliament for a special session to pass the deal. It was during this session, on December 19, 1988, that Paul Martin made his first speech in the House of Commons:

> I am proud to be part of the new wave of Quebec entrepreneurs. This Government has nothing to teach me about the benefits of freer trade … I am a free trader. But we are not debating free trade here; we are debating trade disarmament …

[The Tories] have effectively negated the ability of the Canadian private sector to work with its Government as does the private sector of virtually every other modern state in the world ... We are at an important crossroads. We can either become an economic force with which to be reckoned, with our private sector working in concert with a strong national government, or we will die a slow death as a branch-plant economy with a central government to match. That is what this election was all about.

Martin also said the Liberals would "be there to minimize the harmful effects of this Agreement on our social programs, our agricultural sector, our cultural industries and our environment." In sum, Martin was not opposed to free trade, but to this particular agreement and the laissez-faire model of business–government relations it reflected. And he would live with the agreement but work to ensure that its worst effects were mitigated.

Turner's epic struggle during the election campaign won him the opportunity to make a dignified exit, an option he exercised on April 30, 1989. Leadership speculation had resumed within hours of the 1988 election, and once again Paul Martin's name was among the most prominent. "Paul is my idea of the dream Liberal leader," said former Liberal MP Pierre Deniger, the day after the election. Deniger characterized Martin as "a successful businessman with a social conscience." Marc-Yvan Côté, a senior minister in Premier Bourassa's government, also spoke warmly of the possibility of Martin as federal leader.

Martin did not make a huge impression during his first year as an MP. He was assigned the relatively minor position of housing critic in the Liberal shadow cabinet. He sometimes indulged a tendency to speak off the cuff without regard for party policy, which earned him an indirect but clear reprimand from Turner. And his speaking style failed to excite crowds. But he did carve out some of the territory he was seeking to claim as his own — forward-looking, future-oriented, pro-business but not anti-government, in tune with the new realities of globalization and high technology but not insensitive to social needs:

> This administration claims that its hands are tied by the deficit. That is garbage. Its objectives are not economic, they are ideological, an ideology that went out with the potato famine of the 1840s. The deficit is a problem and it is a very real one, but its solution does not lie in taking a broad axe to our social safety net. Canada has created a network of social programs of which we can be proud. We do not turn our backs on the sick. We do not walk away from the poor. Now, however, the Canadian commitment to social justice is coming under attack.

> Our universities and our whole health care system are under attack, as are our senior citizens. And now, for the first time in our history, the generation of people under thirty is not assured a higher living standard than that enjoyed by their parents. Deficit reduction, yes! But not at any cost, and certainly not without reflection.

Still disorganized and in debt, the Liberal Party was in no hurry to hold a leadership convention. A vote to choose a successor to Turner was eventually called for June 23, 1990, in Calgary. In the meantime, Canada was slowly becoming engulfed in yet another political epic that would reduce the Liberal leadership race to a sideshow and would reach its climax on the very weekend that the vote in Calgary took place, in the midst of one of the most tumultuous years in Canadian political history.

On June 23, 1987, the Quebec National Assembly ratified the constitutional accord reached at Meech Lake in late April and formalized at the Langevin Block in Ottawa in early June. In so doing — at least according to the constitutional interpretation adopted by the Mulroney government and the provincial premiers — it set in motion a three-year period during which every province and the federal Parliament would have to ratify the accord or else it would die. This three-year clock was set to run out on June 23, 1990.

While the Meech Lake Accord generated considerable debate from the beginning, it did not initially seem to be the kind of issue that would shake the country to its foundations. Perhaps this was because, with endorsements from all the provinces and unanimous support in the federal House of Commons, eventual ratification seemed like a foregone conclusion. Then in the fall of 1987, New Brunswick elected an opponent of Meech, Frank McKenna, as its premier. Early in 1988, Howard Pawley's NDP government of Manitoba — itself only a lukewarm supporter of the accord, which Manitoba had yet to ratify — was defeated in the legislature, and the subsequent election brought Gary Filmon to power at the head of a Tory minority government. Filmon continued the Pawley government's fence-sitting policy towards Meech, but the new opposition leader, Sharon Carstairs, was an implacable opponent of the accord, which she pronounced "dead." Nevertheless, Meech barely registered as an issue in the federal election campaign later that year.

Gradually, between late 1988 and early 1990, the country awoke to the large problem that the Meech Lake Accord reflected. In December 1988 the Supreme Court declared the provisions in Quebec's language legislation limiting the use of English on commercial signs contrary to the Charter of Rights. Using the "notwithstanding" clause in the charter, Premier Bourassa's government brought in new legislation, Bill 178, that reestablished most of the original provisions. In distant Winnipeg, Gary Filmon used Bill 178 as his occasion to withdraw his support from the Meech Lake Accord. The connections between Bill 178 and Meech Lake were tenuous. But just as "Watergate" came to mean far more than the burglary at Democratic National Committee headquarters, Meech Lake was becoming a metaphor that encompassed more than the accord itself.

In April 1989 another opponent of the accord, Clyde Wells, was elected premier of Newfoundland, which had ratified the accord under Premier Brian Peckford. In September, Robert Bourassa was easily reelected premier of Quebec — but with a strong enough Parti Québécois opposition to ensure that the sovereignty movement would continue, and with an English-rights group winning several seats in the west end of Montreal. Two months later, Clyde Wells had an angry exchange with Prime Minister Mulroney over Meech at a federal–provincial conference ostensibly called to discuss the economy.

If the Meech Lake Accord was a ticking time bomb for the country, it was all the more so for the Liberal Party, especially since the bomb was programmed to detonate on the very day of the party's leadership vote. With its decentralizing thrust and recognition of Quebec as a distinct society, the accord ran counter to the vision associated with the name of Pierre Elliott Trudeau, which combined an activist central government with a hard line against Quebec nationalism. As a result, the Liberal Party was a natural home for opponents of the accord. McKenna, Carstairs and Wells were all Liberals. Behind them stood two other Liberals: Trudeau himself, who came out of political retirement to speak against the accord, and the heir apparent to the mantle of Trudeau federalism, Jean Chrétien.

Other Liberals believed that even if the Meech Lake Accord represented a departure from the vision that Liberals had held in the past, it was an honourable compromise and as such deserved to be supported. It was time for the party to move on. This view was held especially strongly by a number of Quebec MPs in the Liberal caucus, and it was the one that John Turner, after wavering in the early weeks after the accord was signed, came to endorse. It was also the view of two of the leading candidates to succeed Turner, Sheila Copps and Paul Martin. Martin's campaign, in particular, became a magnet for support-ers of Meech Lake within the Liberal Party. While electing

Chrétien as leader would bring the party at least part way back to Trudeau Liberalism, a Martin victory would represent a greater degree of continuity with the Turner regime. Indeed, Martin was widely believed to be the candidate Turner himself preferred to see as his successor.

Martin's campaign manager was Michael Robinson, an Ottawa lobbyist whom Turner had appointed as the party's chief financial officer after the 1988 election in an effort to clean up the Liberals' financial mess. The campaign's English-Canadian co-chair was Iona Campagnolo, who as a novice MP and junior cabinet minister in the 1970s had been a protégée of Chrétien and Marc Lalonde. Elected party president in 1982 with the support of close Trudeau advisers, she soon fell out with the "PMO crowd" and sought to bridge the party's competing factions. It was a conversation with Campagnolo in February 1984 that persuaded Trudeau that it was time to retire. It was also Campagnolo who, in the Ottawa Civic Centre after Turner's convention victory four months later, called Chrétien up to the podium as the man who "came in second on the ballot, but first in our hearts."

Jean Lapierre, the MP for Shefford, a veteran parliamentarian and former cabinet minister despite being only in his early thirties, was the campaign's Quebec co-chair. In 1982, as a loyal member of Trudeau's Quebec caucus, Lapierre voted for repatriation of the constitution — a vote he later came to regret. He supported Turner during the 1984 leadership campaign, and was rewarded with the fitness and amateur sport portfolio in Turner's short-lived cabinet. In opposition he was in charge of the constitutional dossier for the Liberals. After supporting Turner in the 1986 leadership review, Lapierre became disillusioned and was one of the first to turn to Paul Martin as a possible alternative. Another prominent Martin supporter in Quebec was Gilles Rocheleau, who had been a member of Bourassa's cabinet when Meech Lake was signed and then successfully ran for the federal seat of Hull-Aylmer in 1988.

The Leadership Sideshow

By the time the Liberal leadership campaign began in earnest in January 1990, Meech Lake was a central issue. On January 16, Jean Chrétien — widely acknowledged as the front-runner although he did not officially declare his candidacy for another week — made a major speech on Meech Lake at the University of Ottawa. Chrétien proposed six major amendments to Meech, which in effect amounted to a complete rewriting of the accord and a weakening of its affirmation of Quebec's distinctiveness. The "distinct society" clause would be placed in the preamble rather than as an interpretive clause in the body of the constitution. The listeners, most of whom were students, were split: about half applauded Chrétien, while the other half jeered.

The next day, Paul Martin formally launched his leadership campaign in Montreal, portraying himself as an "unconditional" supporter of Meech Lake and as the candidate of the future rather than the past:

> It may well be that the Liberals are going to have to choose between conflicting visions of this nation, but let me tell you something. If those conflicting visions are one that looks to the future and another one that looks to the past, then there's not much doubt in my mind about which way the Liberal Party is going to go.

Martin directly confronted Chrétien's criticism of the accord: "Mr. Chrétien, by simply rejecting the agreement out of hand and saying that's it, has simply returned us back to zero and is going to make it very difficult under that scenario to obtain a complete constitution."

Martin's campaign launch got favourable notices, but the challenge he faced had several dimensions. He needed to sell his more flexible view of federalism to a party that was still more comfortable with the Trudeau vision of Canada. He needed to find an audience for his ideas about business–government cooperation, which were somewhat removed from the political realities of the moment. And he needed to avoid getting squeezed between the powerful Chrétien machine in front of him and a surprisingly strong Sheila Copps campaign coming up behind him. As a more unequivocal opponent of the free trade agreement than Martin, Copps appealed to the more progressive wing of the party, and in a March Gallup poll asking Canadians whom they preferred as Liberal leader, she came second behind Chrétien, ahead of Martin.

As the campaign proceeded, Martin did not hesitate to distance himself from Trudeau federalism:

> Most Canadians do not feel a contradiction between their desire to function as a member of a given ethnic or cultural community or region of Canada and their desire to be a Canadian. The Trudeau vision would not or could not reconcile those strains, and instead demanded of Canadians that they function as individual rights-bearers relating to a central state ... The main challenge for a post-Trudeau vision of the country is to reconcile the desires of Canadians for a strong national government to express their nationhood and protect their liberty with their genuine aspirations as members of ethnic, cultural and regional groups.

It was precisely this kind of reconciliation that became increasingly difficult in the final months of the Meech Lake ratification period. In February, the Ontario cities of Sault Ste. Marie and Thunder Bay declared themselves unilingually English. Like Quebec's Bill 178 a year earlier, the English-only resolutions (which were replicated in many smaller Ontario municipalities) were not directly related to Canada-wide concerns: They were a response to provincial French-language services legislation and carried the weight of generations-old religious and linguistic disputes. But many Quebecers were quick to see the resolutions as a rejection of Quebec, especially in the light of the growing sentiment in English Canada that the Meech Lake Accord should be watered down.

In March Pierre Trudeau again attacked the accord: "Calling it national reconciliation, Prime Minister Mulroney has in fact been dismantling Canada for the benefit of the provinces." Mulroney appointed a former (and future) cabinet minister, Jean Charest, to chair a parliamentary committee studying possible amendments to Meech. The Quebec National Assembly passed a resolution, supported by both the Liberals and the PQ, insisting that Meech be accepted without changes. The Newfoundland House of Assembly rescinded its ratification of Meech. When the Charest Committee reported in mid-May, its recommendation that Meech be passed as is but then modified through additional amendments was not acceptable to either side. Nor did it please the leading Quebec nationalist minister in Mulroney's cabinet, Lucien Bouchard, who resigned dramatically.

The Liberal leadership campaign did not escape the country's increasingly tense and embittered mood. Martin had not succeeded in overcoming the multiple obstacles that stood between him and the leadership, and Chrétien's lead now appeared insurmountable. He had, however, firmly established himself as the second-place candidate. The simple fact of several competitors grasping for the same prize means that there are strong emotions associated with any leadership campaign, but Meech Lake gave the rivalry between the Martin and Chrétien camps an additional edge. At a policy forum in Montreal on June 3, young Martin supporters characterized Chrétien as a "Judas" and a "vendu" — a sellout. When reports suggested that Chrétien was now prepared to accept Meech Lake, Martin accused him of flip-flopping on the accord. He also suggested that the differences between the two camps might be irreconcilable: "There are a lot of Liberals who are going to say to hell with it."

Chrétien had not turned into a Meech supporter, but he did not want to assume the Liberal leadership among the ashes of

Meech Lake. As Mulroney and the premiers met behind closed doors in Ottawa in a last-ditch effort to save the accord, Chrétien worked privately to create a compromise that would allow the dissident premiers to sign on. By Saturday, June 9, it looked as if Meech had been saved. Frank McKenna had dropped his opposition to the accord early in the week, and now Gary Filmon and Clyde Wells promised to take Meech back to their respective legislatures — in Wells's case, perhaps to a referendum.

But over the next two weeks the accord unravelled again, this time for good. As the deadline approached, Canada's new all-news television channel, CBC Newsworld, moved from St. John's to Quebec City to Ottawa to Winnipeg and back again — and occasionally to Calgary, where the Liberal Party had gathered in convention to choose a new leader. On Thursday evening, June 21, in tones that recalled his crusade against free trade a year and a half earlier, John Turner took his leave with a strong defence of Meech Lake — implicitly criticizing the way Jean Chrétien had handled the issue during the campaign. Chrétien refused to say whether he thought Manitoba and New-foundland should ratify the accord. Pierre Trudeau moved through crowds of admiring Liberals openly arguing that the accord should be killed. Paul Martin privately urged Chrétien supporters to switch to him because he was the candidate who was in tune with Quebec on Meech Lake.

In Winnipeg, Meech ran up against an aboriginal protest movement supported by a Cree member of the legislature, Elijah Harper, who used procedural tactics to prevent a ratifi-cation vote from taking place. In St. John's, at the last minute, Wells called off the free vote in the legislature that he had promised. Late on Friday, June 22, the Tory minister of fed-eral–provincial relations, Lowell Murray, laid the Meech Lake Accord to rest.

The next day, with Martin supporters wearing black arm-bands to mourn the accord, Liberal delegates selected Jean Chrétien as their leader on the first ballot with 57 per cent of the votes. Martin was second with 25 per cent, while Copps was third at a little over 10 per cent. On the convention floor Chrétien warmly greeted one of his leading supporters, Clyde Wells, saying, "Thanks for all you've done, Clyde." While the remark may only have been intended to express gratitude for delivering the Newfoundland delegation to Chrétien, in the context of Wells's role in the demise of Meech Lake it exacerbated the bitterness in the Martin camp. Two of Martin's prominent supporters in Quebec made good on their candidate's earlier suggestion that some Liberals would say, "To hell with it." MPs Jean Lapierre and Gilles Rocheleau walked out of the convention, resigned from the Liberal caucus, and eventually sat with a small group of disillusioned Tories that formed around Lucien Bouchard. Later in the summer, this group formed itself into a political party, the Bloc Québécois, the first party favouring Quebec sovereignty to be represented in the federal House of Commons. Lapierre served as the Bloc's house leader until he left electoral politics in 1992 to become a radio talk-show host.

Environmental Enthusiast

While Lapierre and Rocheleau did not feel that there was any room for them in a Chrétien-led Liberal Party, the same was not true of Paul Martin. At a caucus meeting the day after the leadership vote, Chrétien came down from the podium to bring Martin up with him. It was a preliminary indication that the two candidates who had criticized each other so vigorously during the leadership campaign would now work together to bring the Liberal Party to power.

Both Chrétien and Martin are intensely pragmatic politicians, and they recognized from the outset that they needed each other. As the second-place finisher, Martin could aspire to a senior cabinet portfolio if Chrétien became prime minister. From Chrétien's vantage point, the circumstances in which he assumed the leadership of the party meant that he could use all the help he could get. The Liberals were badly divided, deeply in debt and unsure of their direction. The Meech Lake compromise that Chrétien had hoped for had not materialized. As a result of his anti–Meech Lake stance, the new leader was especially weak in his native Quebec, where Martin could be useful in rebuilding his credibility.

If the Liberals had any consolation, it was that the governing Tories were in even worse shape. But disenchanted Tory supporters had an increasing range of options. In the west, they were far less likely to turn to the Liberals than to Preston Manning's uppity Reform Party, whose first MP, Deborah Grey, was elected in a 1989 by-election. In Quebec, an August 1990 by-election in downtown Montreal called to fill a seat left vacant by the death of popular Liberal MP Jean-Claude Malépart resulted in a decisive victory for Bloc Québécois candidate Gilles Duceppe, promising a bright future for Lucien Bouchard's new formation. The by-election loss reduced the Liberals' Quebec caucus to a historic low of nine members. Chrétien's old bailiwick of Saint-Maurice was held by a Tory, and he needed to look to New Brunswick for a safe seat to run in. Only Ontario and the Atlantic provinces appeared to be fertile Liberal territory. Furthermore, the new leader's office was not running smoothly, and in early 1991 he faced health problems that kept him on the sidelines for an extended period.

Martin settled into the new and more prominent role that his showing in the leadership campaign had secured for him. He was appointed environment critic, a major responsibility at a time when environmental consciousness was at its peak, and associate finance critic. In the wake of the UN-sponsored Brundtland Report, the drought of 1988, and scary scenarios surrounding global warming and the thinning of the ozone layer — and in the buildup to the Earth Summit in Rio de Janeiro in 1992 presided over by his onetime Power Corporation mentor Maurice Strong — the environment provided Martin with a prominent platform.

His thinking about the environment reflected his overall philosophy. He became a passionate environmentalist as he consistently upheld the Brundtland Commission's notion of "sustainable development," criticized of the government for its inaction, and advocated a more interventionist approach to the environment. When the North American Free Trade Agreement came before the House, he roundly criticized its environmental provisions for being too weak:

> There should be: first, clear principles for the harmonization of environmental standards between all countries in the agreement; second, a clear commitment that the objective of this harmonization should be to establish the highest level of environmental protection; third, the incorporation of environmental considerations openly and publicly in the dispute settlement resolution process; and fourth, the establishment of an environmental threshold for new country accession to the agreement.

Moreover, he defined the issue of the Rio summit in the following terms: "Will the focus of international trade shift from raw market forces to the needs of sustainable development?" However, he shied away from the suggestion that business, in general terms, was responsible for environmental degradation. When NDP member Len Taylor introduced a bill of environmental rights in the House in 1991, Martin supported the initiative but distanced himself from Taylor's criticism of business:

> I do not believe that it was necessary in presenting this bill, which as he so properly said should involve all members of the House and indeed all of the Canadian people, for him to engage in a particularly blanket and vicious attack on Canadian entrepreneurs. It is not fair and it is not appropriate.
>
> I am sure that if he were to review his remarks, he would really understand that it is not all business, not all of the

private sector, that engages in unlawful pollution. Yes, there are some businesses which do so and they should indeed suffer penalties. Let us not engage in universal condemnation.

As Martin saw it, the economy and the environment are integrally related and there is no contradiction between economic and envirnonmental objectives:

> You simply cannot have a strong economy if you do not make protection of the environment your number one priority ... I would suggest to members on the other side of the House that they take a look at West Germany and ask themselves why it is that West Germany is both the environmental leader of Europe as well as the economic leader of Europe. It is no coincidence. One follows the other.

Meanwhile, as associate finance critic, Martin continued to criticize the government for trying to solve the deficit through program cuts:

> When this government came to power, it had one goal: deficit reduction. It has failed miserably. Why? Because of its failure to understand that deficit reduction does not only come from cutting; it comes from growth, and growth comes from investment. This government has consistently under-invested while other countries in the world, such as Germany and Japan, have invested. Those countries now prosper while Michael Wilson has brought this country to its knees.

Repairing the Business Link

Martin was very much involved in the efforts to renew and reposition the Liberal Party that began soon after Chrétien assumed the leadership. While Martin's public speeches had a left-liberal tinge to them, his activities within the party were directed towards repairing its ties with business that had been so badly frayed by the Liberal anti–free trade campaign of 1988. In this endeavour he made common cause with two other Liberal MPs: John Manley, an Ottawa lawyer and former chair of the Ottawa Board of Trade, and Roy MacLaren, a Toronto advertising executive and magazine publisher who had served briefly in the Trudeau and Turner cabinets. The "three M's" (who would all end up with major economic portfolios once the Liberals took office in 1993) aimed to provide the Liberals with an economic platform that was more suited to the times.

The times were difficult ones. Just as Canada was faced with the challenge of adjusting to the effects of the free trade agreement, it entered a major recession, exacerbated by Ottawa's spending cuts in the name of deficit reduction and by the anti-inflation rigidity of the Bank of Canada under John Crow (see chapter 4). Furthermore, the recession reduced government revenues while the high interest rates associated with Crow's policy augmented debt service charges, so that Canadians suffered the pain associated with a war on the deficit without enjoying any of the gain.

The early 1990s were also the time when the word *globalization* became an economic and political mantra. While the term was invoked to explain an improbably wide range of phenomena and often served as a substitute for analysis, it did reflect a growing awareness that something fundamental was shifting in world trade relations and in the relationship between corporations and the national governments that seek to regulate them. Unlike the free trade agreement in 1988, globalization was not an issue that admitted of a simple yes/no answer. There were suggestions, at one extreme, that Canada reject globalization and retreat into sturdy self-reliance. At the other end of the spectrum — which included elements within the governing Conservatives — the proper response to globalization was simply for governments to get out of the way and allow market forces to do their work. Most of the Liberal Party found itself somewhere in between.

As the owner of a major corporation that he had led into the global marketplace, and as a politician who had attacked specific provisions of the free trade agreement without opposing free trade in principle, Paul Martin was a Liberal to whom a positive response to globalization came naturally. His major concern was with the best way for Canada to compete in the new global environment. Starting in 1991, he and like-minded Liberals got the opportunity to advance their priorities.

The Liberals' effort to revamp their economic policies began in earnest at a thinkers' conference in Aylmer, Quebec, in November 1991, where the keynote speaker was one of Martin's favourite economic theoreticians, Lester Thurow of the Massachusetts Institute of Technology. Thinkers' conferences have a high standing in the folk memory of the Liberal Party. The classic of the genre was the Kingston Conference of September 1960 (see chapter 1), where the Liberals sought to cast off the tired image that still clung to them from the later Saint-Laurent years and reinvent themselves as a forward-looking party. The ideas discussed at Kingston, generally directed towards expanding Canada's welfare state, were fashioned into resolutions at a 1961 policy convention and then into a party platform for the 1962 and 1963 elections.

When the Liberals tried to repeat the formula, as they did several times over the next few decades, it was mostly to distance themselves from the legacy of Kingston. At Harrison Hot Springs, B.C., in 1969, the party formulated a slightly harder-edged Liberalism for the new Trudeau era, deciding that it was not in the government's capacity to eliminate poverty. In 1977, at an airport hotel near Toronto, the party sought to effect a more radical change of course and fashion a new Trudeau to run against the interventionist Trudeau of the previous decade. However, the Liberals lost the 1979 election, and when a twist of fate brought them back to office in 1980, Trudeau regarded his good fortune as an opportunity to have one last interventionist kick at the can. Not even the accession to the leadership in 1984 of the paradigmatic business Liberal, John Turner, brought about the long-awaited change. With Turner's laissez-faire leadership style, a small caucus whose more prominent members tended towards social Liberalism, and a Tory government that left little room for opposition from the right, the Liberals found themselves further removed from their one-time corporate allies than ever before.

In the early 1990s, it was Paul Martin and his colleagues who inherited the task of bringing the party back to a more centrist Liberalism on the pre-Kingston model of Louis Saint-Laurent and C.D. Howe, in which government was both closely allied with business and active in shaping society. While there were different views within the party on what direction the Liberals should take, there was general agreement that the party needed some kind of direction. The sense of drift that had pervaded the Turner years and carried over into the early months of Chrétien's leadership had still not dissipated. Chrétien was widely regarded as a disappointment and was still deeply unpopular in Quebec. Some of the passions that had surrounded Meech Lake had faded, but new divisions had opened up over how best to respond to the global economy.

Speaker after speaker at the Aylmer conference highlighted the need for the Liberals to come to terms with globalization. "Globalization is not right-wing or left-wing," Chrétien said in his closing speech. "It is simply a fact of life." Lester Thurow — like Paul Martin a believer in an active role for government in the context of globalization — also made it clear that in his view there was no alternative to being a player in the global economy. He presented Japan as a model of how the game can be played successfully. Not everyone was persuaded that ac-commodation to the global economy was either inevitable or a good idea. For Lloyd Axworthy, the Winnipeg MP who had been one of the leaders in moving the caucus to the left in the Turner period, all the talk about globalization was "just a cover for right-wing ideology." For Paul Martin, however, Aylmer set the Liberals on a course that he could be comfortable with. The party would not oppose globalization but would seek to turn it to Canada's advantage by investing in human resources and by emphasizing economic sectors where Canada could compete in global markets.

As had happened after Kingston three decades earlier, the Liberals followed Aylmer with a policy convention, held in Ottawa in February 1992, and then with the crafting of an election platform. Martin was named co-chair of the platform committee, along with party research director Chaviva Hošek, whose inclination was more towards social Liberalism and whose varied background included academia, business, the presidency of the National Action Committee on the Status of Women and the housing portfolio in the Ontario government of David Peterson. Martin and Hošek toured the country twice, gathering input from fellow Liberals and other Canadians. They disagreed frequently on policy questions, but eventually worked out a set of proposals that were refined into a party platform.

Victory by the Red Book

Meanwhile, the Tory government entered its final stages of self-destruction. In the summer of 1992, against all expectations, a constitutional agreement was reached that gained the support of the federal government, ten provinces, two territories and four Native organizations. After a symbolic signing ceremony in Charlottetown in late August, the agreement was put to a referendum scheduled for October 26. The two main opposition parties in the Commons, the Liberals and the NDP, also supported the agreement, and on September 9 Paul Martin rose in the House of Commons to praise it as an "honourable compromise" that was "in line with a tradition of great historical compromises that made it possible for Canada to become a nation, to develop and to be respected and envied by all the peoples of the earth."

However, dissenting voices soon arose. It was only to be expected that Quebec sovereignists would oppose the agreement, but others soon joined them for reasons of their own: from the right, the Reform Party under Preston Manning; from the left, the National Action Committee on the Status of Women under Judy Rebick; from the past, former prime minister Pierre Trudeau. On October 26 the Charlettetown Accord went down to defeat, and with it sank Brian Mulroney's last hope of political rehabilitation. In February 1993 he announced his resignation. The Tories needed a new leader who could rejuvenate the party just as Pierre Trudeau had given new life to the fading Liberals in 1968, and they appeared to have found such a person in Kim Campbell, like Trudeau a reform-minded justice minister, whom they elected leader at a June convention. Campbell promised to do politics differently and briefly brought the Tories back to the top of the polls. On September 8, 1993, she called an election.

A week into the campaign, the Liberals released the results of the work of Martin and Hošek's platform committee in the form of an attractively laid out book with a red cover, which rapidly became known as the Red Book. Publishing the platform as a single document, rather than through staged policy announcements as parties generally did, was widely regarded as a high-risk strategy. While the Liberals, virtually neck and neck with the Tories in the polls, were by no means assured of victory in an unpredictable five-party race (there was much speculation about the election resulting in a fragmented "pizza Parliament"), they did have a strong possibility of forming the next government. The other parties were on the lookout for targets to aim at, and the Red Book seemed to offer such a target.

But in the end the Red Book, which Chrétien brandished at virtually every campaign stop, was an important element in the Liberals' successful campaign. It created the impression that they had a plan for the country, established a sense of accountability by providing a way for voters to measure their performance once they were in office, gave Liberal candidates with divergent ideological tendencies a common policy base to refer to, and staked out political territory where Canadians tend to be most comfortable: in the centre.

The Red Book contained proposals for an apprenticeship program, a Canadian technology network and additional child care spaces (this last, in deference to Martin's budgetary concerns, to be implemented only in each year following a year of at least 3 per cent economic growth). It had a whole chapter on one of Martin's favourite topics, sustainable development. And it was studiously vague about two Tory-sponsored measures on which the Liberals had been critical but had no real alternatives to propose: the Goods and Services Tax and the extension of free trade to Mexico in the form of the North American Free Trade Agreement. Its most consequential sections, however, dealt with the deficit and economic growth.

The Liberals' proposal for priming the economic pump, the infrastructure program, had already been announced. The $2 billion representing the federal share of this program would be additional expenditure and hence add to the deficit. But the Liberals did not see promoting growth and fighting the deficit as contradictory. As the Red Book put it,

> A Liberal government will adopt a two-track fiscal policy, matching a drive for jobs and growth with a comprehensive approach to controlling debt and deficits. The two tracks run parallel: fiscal discipline will support economic growth, while growth and jobs will enhance government revenues.

Martin explained just after the Red Book's release that high unemployment and the high national debt had the same root cause: economic decline. And there was a role for government in reversing that decline. "Economic growth," Martin said on September 20, "is not a matter for market forces alone." On the deficit, Martin had wanted the Liberals to promise a balanced budget (as the Tories and the Reform Party did). The more cautious Chrétien preferred to avoid such a rigid target. As a result, the Red Book committed the Liberals to the "immediate goal" of reducing the deficit to 3 per cent of Gross Domestic Product (a standard set by the member states of the European Union in the 1992 Maastricht Treaty) by the end of their third year in office. In addition, the Liberals insisted that they were not interested in deficit reduction for its own sake. The Red Book quoted Nobel laureate James Tobin (originator of the proposed Tobin Tax on international financial transactions), an economist whose work Martin particularly admired at the time:

> Deficit reduction is not an end in itself. Its rationale is to improve productivity, real wages, and living standards of our children and their children. If the measures to cut deficits actually diminish GDP, raise unemployment, and reduce future-oriented activities of government, business, and households, they do not achieve the goals that are their raison d'être: rather they retard them.

After the release of the Red Book, the Liberals began to open up a lead in the polls, and this lead widened as the campaign progressed. The Tories declined more precipitously than anyone had predicted — so far and so fast that the projected "pizza Parliament" did not materialize and the country elected a majority Liberal government instead.

In Quebec, the Tory collapse meant that the election was a two-way struggle between the Liberals and the Bloc Québécois. On a Quebec-wide basis, the *Bloquistes* won this struggle decisively, but there were pockets of Liberal strength, the main one being the western half of Montreal Island, which includes Martin's constituency of LaSalle–Émard. Once again Martin received substantial corporate donations — $2,000 from Redpath Sugar, $2,000 from Lévesque Beaubien Geoffrion, $1,500 from McCain Foods — although overall campaign contributions were down somewhat from 1988. With LaSalle–Émard's significant non-francophone population, the Bloc was not a serious threat in the riding.

On election day, October 25, Martin defeated the Bloc candidate, twenty-three-year-old Éric Cimon, by more than 13,000 votes, with the Tories a distant third. With 176 other Liberals also elected (ninety-eight of them in Ontario), he was now part of the governing party and high on the list of potential appointees to the cabinet, most likely in a major economic portfolio. In the House of Commons, the leadership campaign and the platform committee, he had passionately advanced ideas for bringing Canada's economy up to date and making it work in the new global era. Now he would get the chance to implement those ideas.

CHAPTER FOUR

Slaying the Deficit Monster

.D. Howe, the powerful entrepreneur-politician of the
King and Saint-Laurent eras, held a series of economic
portfolios in his twenty-two years in government: marine and railways, transport, munitions and supply, reconstruc-
tion, defence production, trade and commerce. In these
portfolios he had the opportunity to run big things — Canada's
broadcasting infrastructure, war industries and atomic energy
program along with crown corporations such as Polymer and
his beloved Trans-Canada Airlines — as well as have a broad
influence on the Canadian economy as a whole.

Paul Martin saw himself as being in the same mould as
Howe. He wanted to be an economic superminister in the Howe
tradition, someone who would direct government and business
in working together to create a growing, prosperous Canadian
economy. He believed he could play such a role as minister of
industry, a portfolio that incorporated parts of Howe's old
bailiwicks. But the situation had changed drastically since
Howe's time. The big thing now was the deficit — big both in
numerical terms (well over $30 billion even by Tory estimates)
and in the psychological hold it had on official Ottawa, led by
the civil servants in the department of finance. Even during
Mulroney's last term, an astute Ottawa observer had said, "The

tyranny of Finance has never been stronger than it is now." This "tyranny" was about to become stronger still.

In 1993, in this context of fiscal constraint, there was no room for an economic superminister with big ideas. There was, however, room for a strong finance minister who would tame the deficit monster. After considerable hesitation, Martin accepted Jean Chrétien's request that he take on the finance portfolio. Immediately after being sworn into the cabinet, he flew to Windsor to be at the bedside of his dying mother. Nell Martin awoke to see her two children, Paul and Mary-Ann, standing at her bedside. "Why?" she asked. Paul started to reply that they were there because she was ill and they had come to see her. "No," she said, cutting him off. "Why finance?"

As an opposition MP, Martin had been critical of Tory efforts to cut the deficit by reducing spending. As minister of finance, he would make the war against the deficit his own, and it was as a deficit-cutter that he would make his mark. Persuaded by his officials that bringing the deficit down was the top priority, he became a very effective advocate for this course of action. Martin's achievement was twofold: fiscal and political. He not only brought the deficit down but did so at modest political cost to the Liberal government. Arguably, the political achievement was the greater of the two. The devastating defeat of the Tories stood as a warning of the fate that can await governments that take the axe to cherished programs in the name of deficit reduction. There was no broad acceptance of the need for an attack on the deficit through program cuts. Martin's own previous speeches, and the campaign positions of the Liberal Party, had not made the new finance minister's task any easier.

Both the fiscal problem and the political one had deep roots, stretching back to choices made during Canada's postwar economic boom and government responses to more uncertain economic times in the 1970s. It is far too simplistic to treat the debt as a straightforward consequence of federal fiscal irresponsibility, in the manner of *Globe and Mail* columnist Jeffrey Simpson:

> What fools Canadian governments were for a quarter of a century, beginning with the nightmarish fiscal management of prime minister Pierre Trudeau. Deficits, deficits and nothing but deficits from the early 1970s on, year in and year out, in good times and bad, ran up a staggering national debt.

The story of the growth of the great Canadian debt is one with no heroes and few villains — at least not the expected ones. To understand the challenges that faced Paul Martin in his new position as finance minister, a recounting of this story provides some useful background.

The Great Canadian Debt

In the three decades following the end of the Second World War, the Canadian economy grew rapidly with what seemed almost effortless ease. During this period, government economic policies were based largely on the theories of John Maynard Keynes, who has become both one of the most admired and one of the most reviled figures in twentieth-century economics. For his critics, the term "Keynesian economics" has become a kind of shorthand for rampant state interventionism in the economy, profligate overspending, gargantuan deficits and a crushing debt load.

Keynes's theory, first proposed during the Great Depression of the 1930s, clearly did advocate deficit spending. During periods of recession, extra state spending could provide a much-needed stimulus for growth. But there was an important corollary to this: Governments should run surpluses during periods of expansion to create a cushion to deal with the next, inevitable downturn. Many of those who take such glee in disparaging the legacy of Keynes seem to forget that he sought to balance deficits in some years with surpluses in others.

During the Second World War, Keynes's ideas proved their worth amply. To finance a huge and unprecedented military buildup, governments spent money they didn't actually have. Among the achievements of this policy was a great economic boom in countries such as Canada that participated actively in the war without having to fight on their own soil. Once the bugaboos associated with deficit spending had been cast aside, the Canadian government found itself in a position to lay the foundations of a welfare state that quickly overtook Franklin D. Roosevelt's New Deal provisions in the United States.

Throughout the 1950s and 1960s, Ottawa was able to keep its books almost in balance, but not completely. In some years there were minor surpluses, while in other years spending on government programs and the public debt were higher than revenues. Deficits were more common than surpluses, but they were always well below 3 per cent of GDP (the target Paul Martin would set for the Liberals in 1993) until the mid-1970s, and the accumulated public debt rose more slowly than the size of the economy nearly every year. Ottawa had ended the Second World War deeply in hock, with a total debt of nearly $12.6 billion in 1947. This may sound minuscule in today's terms, but it represented an amount equal to 103.5 per cent of gross domestic product. Five years later the debt still stood at $10.4 billion, but this represented only 45.7 per cent of GDP. After that, the debt began rising again in dollar terms, but only at a modest rate, and it declined steadily as a proportion of GDP, falling to as low as 18.4 per cent in 1975.

The beginning of Ottawa's string of rising deficits was contained in the 1973 budget presented by then Finance Minister John Turner, who forecast a deficit in the range of $2 billion. Members of the Progressive Conservative opposition, ostensibly the right-thinking guardians of fiscal rectitude, launched an attack on Turner, not because they said it was wrong to use a bit of pump-priming to get the economy moving more quickly, but because the deficit was not high enough. A hardy seed that Turner planted in this budget and that would haunt future finance ministers was to index personal benefits such as old-age pensions to inflation while de-indexing personal income taxes. In other words, he almost guaranteed that public spending would rise more quickly than government revenues, at least until the de-indexing provision was removed in 1986. Even under the rosy economic growth scenarios that had prevailed in previous decades, this would spell fiscal trouble, and the scenarios were no longer so rosy.

The first truly perceptible sign that good economic times would not last forever came in 1973 when a sudden jump in world oil prices showed the incipient fragility of the American-led international economic system. The second oil shock, in 1979, was far more devastating in its effects, and that awful word "stagflation," coined a few years earlier, became common currency. This dismal combination of stagnant output and high inflation led to a pronounced rise in government deficits and higher government borrowing requirements.

At first this did not appear especially alarming. Over the years, as we have seen, Canada was able to bring its postwar debt down to comfortable levels. A little extra borrowing, and a little extra debt, did not seem such terrifying prospects. As the years went by, this little mound of additional debt became a rather sizeable mountain, exacerbated by the short but very sharp 1981–82 recession. The federal debt climbed past $50 billion in 1977, past $100 billion in 1980, and past $200 billion in 1985. Part of this increase was due to inflation, but even in GDP-related terms the debt rose from a low of 18.4 per cent in 1975 to 46.3 per cent ten years later, and it just kept rising. Public debt charges during this same period ballooned from $3.2 billion to $22.4 billion, or as a proportion of GDP from 2.1 per cent to 5.2 per cent.

By the time of the 1984 federal election campaign, John Turner had resurfaced in politics, this time as leader of the Liberal Party and, for a forgettable three months, as prime minister of Canada. The opposition Tories had lost their earlier indulgence — or so they let on — for stimulative deficits. Both before and after sweeping to power at the polls under Brian Mulroney in 1984, they loudly bewailed the almost $200-billion accumulated debt that the Liberals had bestowed on the country. The Conservative legacy, they proclaimed, was going to be different.

Keynesianism in Reverse

The new finance minister was Michael Wilson, a Toronto-area MP who arrived with impeccable Bay Street credentials as former head of Dominion Securities, Canada's biggest stock brokerage firm (later taken over by the Royal Bank of Canada). With these credentials, Wilson was seemingly a far more likely candidate for the role of effective deficit-fighter than Paul Martin would be nine years later. He was praised in the financial press as someone with a superb grasp of numbers who could get his mind around the intricate fiscal scenarios some of the mandarins in his department seemed to enjoy concocting. One area where his grasp may have been somewhat weaker, however, was basic economics.

The Tories came to power at a moment when the last lingering effects of the early-1980s recession were sinking into memory. These were boom times. The economy was showing robust growth, unemployment was falling, and almost anybody who invested money in the stock market or in real estate seemed to be coming out well ahead. According to Keynesian theory, it is under favourable conditions such as these that governments should be putting their fiscal houses in order, to prepare for a rainy day. In practical terms, this means looking for ways to cut spending while holding taxes steady or, alternatively, to keep spending stable while raising taxes. But Keynes had fallen out of favour. South of the border, supply-side economics was all the rage. In the United States, taxes had fallen, consumers were spending, and nobody seemed to care much that the national debt was swelling.

Wilson faced conflicting pressures. He was certainly well aware of the twin debt and deficit problems, but he and the officials whose advice he most trusted were concerned that a sizeable contraction in government spending or a failure to lower taxes in line with what was happening in Reagan's Washington could suck growth out of the economy and hasten the arrival of a period of stagnation or, worse yet, recession. He also faced pressure from his Bay Street peers and from the investors they dealt with — people who were profiting handsomely from the stock market and real estate booms, especially in southern Ontario — to go lighter on effective capital gains taxes, which were already lower than taxes on earned income.

In his first budget, presented in 1985, Wilson announced a massive giveaway to the wealthy, providing a lifetime tax exemption on up to $500,000 in capital gains. This exemption was subsequently lowered to $100,000, which meant that benefits were no longer quite as heavily skewed to the wealthy, but many of them had already taken advantage of the maximum allowance in any case. (One of Paul Martin's first moves as finance minister was to eliminate this lifetime exemption entirely.) In his first and subsequent budgets, Wilson also announced reductions in personal income tax, with the biggest cuts going to those with the biggest incomes. Not only did this produce a less progressive income tax, but it also limited the government's ability to tame the deficit.

There are two ways, of course, to reduce deficits. One is to raise taxes, and the other is to cut spending. The idea of raising taxes is anathema to supply-siders, who argue that higher taxes lead to slower growth and thus fail to produce the desired increase in revenues. Spending cuts present their own problems, the most significant of which is that the people who benefit from spending do not like to see it reduced. The Mulroney government, noting that the elderly, on average, were better off than ever before while many wage-earners had failed to keep up with inflation, toyed with the idea of a partial de-indexation of old-age pensions, which would have spelled a slow decline in the value of pensions even with moderate inflation. A single, well-organized demonstration on Parliament Hill caused the government to lose its nerve, and the idea was quickly abandoned. It may not have been a very good idea to begin with, at least in the form in which it was presented, but it demonstrated to Mulroney and his cabinet just how difficult it was going to be to rein in spending.

The 1985–86 fiscal year, the first period with the Tories fully in control, showed a slight drop in program spending, to $86.1 billion from $87.1 billion the year before. But soon spending was on the rise again, reaching $122.6 billion in 1992–93 near the end of the Tory reign. At 17.5 per cent of GDP, this was almost as high in real terms as the levels late in the Trudeau era that the Tories had found so excessive when they sat on the opposition benches.

Rapid economic growth in the middle and late 1980s kept revenues on the rise despite the Wilson tax cuts, and the federal deficit declined from the Liberal-inherited $38.4 billion in 1984–85 to $27.8 billion in 1987–88. These were still big numbers, however. Here was a government running massive deficits even in boom times. The accumulated debt continued its inexorable rise, passing $300 billion in March 1988, despite the perpetual blather from Mulroney and Wilson about their valiant attacks on the deficit. Nor did it fail to escape notice that an ever higher portion of government spending, by now more than 30 per cent, was going to service the debt.

In 1987–88, the federal government actually showed an operating surplus, a modest $1.16 billion, meaning that revenues were higher than program spending. This was the first operating surplus since 1974–75. But with public debt charges of nearly $29 billion in 1987–88, this operating surplus paled into insignificance. Even after the operating surplus grew to almost $10.6 billion in 1990–91, it was dwarfed by debt charges of $42.6 billion. The government and the public that pays for it were running on a treadmill that kept going faster.

Two main reasons explain why debt service rose so quickly. One is that accumulated debt kept climbing and interest had to be paid on ever larger sums. But a more fundamental reason in the late 1980s was the sharp rise in Canadian interest rates engineered by John Crow, governor of the Bank of Canada, who established for himself an unrivalled reputation as an anti-inflation zealot. Inflation was not nearly as serious a concern as it had been a few years earlier, but levels were slightly higher in Canada than in some of its G-7 partners. Low inflation was considered in many economic circles to be a prerequisite for long-term growth, although there were plenty of dissenting voices.

There had been fears that the stock market crash of October 1987 portended an imminent recession, but this turned out to be merely one more example of how divorced the securities markets can often be from economic reality. Two more years of strong growth lay ahead. In southern Ontario the economy was performing so robustly that the central bank perceived an imminent overheating, which could lead to a jump in inflation. Tighter controls on the money supply led inevitably to higher interest rates, which put a damper on economic growth not only in southern Ontario but in most other parts of Canada as well, including vast areas of the country where the threat of economic overheating was close to nil and where unemployment remained the key economic concern.

In 1990 Canada entered a recession from which it was not to emerge until about 1994, using anecdotal evidence as a guide — even if standard economic indicators pointed to an earlier end. The Canadian recession started sooner and ended later than the U.S. recession of the early 1990s. Although it was less severe than the 1981–82 recession, its great length and the double-digit unemployment rates it created and perpetuated cast a weary pall on most of Canada (though British Columbia seemed largely to escape its effects).

Crow remained unrepentant to the end, but in fairness it should be noted that his actions formed only one part of the equation. Simply put, Canada was caught in a mismatch between fiscal policy and monetary policy. Although the finance department and its political masters claimed to support the

Bank of Canada's rigid inflation targets, there was a tug-of-war between them, even if it was not perceived as such. On the one hand, the central bank was aiming to destimulate the economy, and it actually saw higher unemployment as a desirable goal insofar as it calmed inflationary pressures. On the other hand, federal and provincial governments were reluctant to raise taxes or lower spending, fearing the harmful effects on employment that the central bank countenanced with such equanimity. Governments also knew that higher unemployment would cut into revenues and worsen the deficits they had become so intent on lowering. And they were abundantly aware that high unemployment makes voters unhappy. Ottawa's twin financial authorities were tugging in opposite directions. In their dissonant measures aimed at fighting inflation and deficits simultaneously, they left hundreds of thousands of Canadians needlessly unemployed.

The Bank of Canada has often been accused of recklessness in failing to take the human consequences of its actions into account but, again, the recklessness was not all on one side. A case in point is the Liberal government in Ontario, from 1985 to 1990, led by David Peterson, who kept spending money without restraint even as the economy in Canada's industrial and financial heartland seemed to be on the point of overheating. This went beyond any sensible notion of stimulative spending. Much of the Bob Rae deficit, for which the post-1990 New Democratic government took everlasting blame, was merely an extension of the David Peterson deficit. Peterson truly was one of the progenitors of the great Canadian recession.

At the federal level, deficits dipped only slightly even amid the boom times of the late 1980s and then started rising again as the recession cut into revenues and led to higher spending on unemployment relief. The accumulated debt passed the $400-billion mark in 1991 and the half-trillion mark soon after Paul Martin became finance minister near the end of 1993, peaking a couple of years later at 71.9 per cent of gross domestic product.

The Mulroney government became more serious about fighting the deficit only as Canada was about to enter its long recession. In his 1989 budget Michael Wilson announced extensive spending cuts. Among them were reductions in Via Rail passenger train service for which the government paid a political price that was out of proportion to the actual importance of passenger trains in day-to-day transport patterns. Even some people who would not normally take the train felt a sense of loss when service was discontinued to cities stretching from Regina to Trois-Rivières to Sydney, and when the fabled western transcontinental service was reduced to three trains a week.

The cuts affected many other programs as well. They were also emblematic of a fundamental misunderstanding of economic theory by Wilson and his colleagues. It should be obvious that the time to run big deficits is not when the economy is surging ahead. And the time to look for drastic savings is not when the economy can use extra stimulus. Canada's debt and deficit problems cannot be blamed on the teachings of John Maynard Keynes. What Wilson and Mulroney applied was not Keynesian economics. Rather, it was Keynesian economics in reverse. Therein lies a tragedy of significant proportions.

As if this misapplication of Keynesian theory and the accompanying mismatch of monetary and fiscal policy were not bad enough, Wilson also committed a serious and repeated political blunder (a blunder Paul Martin would take pains not to repeat) by consistently underestimating the extent of the budgetary deficit. Year after year, the deficit forecasts contained in Wilson's budgets were lower, often far lower, than the shortfalls that actually materialized. Each time this happened, of course, Wilson lost a little more credibility, not least among his Bay Street acolytes. And each time the Tories added to the federal debt, the sum that had to be applied towards interest payments rose geometrically as the size of the debt increased and the upward pressure on interest rates was intensified. Canadian public finances were caught in a nasty spiral.

In sum, the huge growth of the debt in relation to gross domestic product occurred to a large extent in three big jumps. The first, in the late 1970s, was a result of fairly standard Keynesian operating deficits and in the normal course of events could have been corrected through operating surpluses. Instead, however, a second and more serious jump took place in the early 1980s, brought on both by high interest rates and by recession-induced operating deficits. The third jump, in the early 1990s, was caused almost entirely by the high interest rates associated with John Crow's anti-inflation campaign.

As large, as longstanding and as complex as the problems facing Paul Martin were in 1993, the conditions for dealing with these problems were about to get better. In the early years of Martin's tenure, Canada climbed out of the depths of the recession, inflation was negligible, and interest rates fell. The political circumstances were more favourable as well. There was no party that could mount an effective and credible attack on Martin from the left, at least in English Canada; in Quebec the Bloc Québécois upheld the traditional social democratic position that deficit reduction should not come at the expense of social programs. Furthermore, in contrast to previous parliaments, there was no opposition party that represented a serious alternative to the government.

So Paul Martin's hand was not without its strong cards. But when he took over the finance portfolio from Don Mazankowski, Wilson's immediate successor, it remained to be seen just how strong they would be, and how well he would play them.

Struggle for Martin's Soul?

When he became finance minister, Martin was already familiar with the burdens that compound interest can impose. His takeover of Canada Steamship Lines had been achieved through a leveraged buyout, and leveraged buyouts by definition involve high levels of debt. Anybody who has to deal with large amounts of debt becomes aware very quickly of the ballooning effects of compound interest. The bigger the debt, the faster it grows unless you are running a profit (in business parlance) or a surplus (in government) that can be applied to pay down principal. Even after the Tories achieved an operating surplus in the 1987–88 fiscal year (which turned into an operating deficit four years later as the recession bit into revenues), public debt charges continued to rise because the government had to continue paying interest on the interest as well as on the principal. An even bigger reason was the tight-money policies imposed by John Crow at the Bank of Canada. A very tight fist on the growth of the money supply had pushed interest rates to record or near-record highs when adjusted for inflation, making borrowing very expensive for Canadian businesses and individuals alike.

One problem Martin did not have to contend with was inflation. John Crow's painful medicine had squeezed much of the lifeblood out of the economy, leading to a prolonged period of double-digit unemployment in Canada even after the United States economy moved into a period of vigorous growth starting in 1992. With many Canadians out of work and millions more fearful of being put on the dole at short notice, consumer spending slowed to very cautious levels, wages stagnated, and inflationary pressures were effectively doused, obviously at a heavy cost. Crow, with explicit support from the government, had set a target of between 1 and 3 per cent annual increases in the consumer price index. From 1983 to 1991, inflation had been stuck at between 4 and 6 per cent annually — an improvement, certainly, over the preceding ten years when the annual rate had never dipped below 7.5 per cent and had climbed as high as 12.4 per cent in 1981. Beginning in 1992, Canada truly became a low-inflation country. In fact, from 1992 to 1997, the consumer price index as measured by Statistics Canada rose only 7.6 per cent — not annually, but for that entire five-year period. In 1994, prices rose only 0.2 per cent, based on a monthly average. Although interest rates did start falling in 1991, it took longer for the cost of borrowing in Canada to come down to U.S. levels. And the single biggest borrower was the government of Canada.

One of Martin's first moves as finance minister was to sack John Crow. This was not the messy sort of business that John Diefenbaker encountered when he set out to dump Bank of Canada governor James Coyne in the wake of disagreements over monetary policy. Fortunately for Martin, Crow was nearing the end of his first seven-year term as governor. It is traditional for the governor to serve two terms, and during that time the governor can act, in theory at least, independently of the government. Martin had several meetings with Crow, and accounts of these meetings suggest that the two of them simply failed to hit it off.

Crow had a well-deserved reputation for arrogance. He had seemingly gone out of his way to antagonize Liberal MPs, including Martin, at parliamentary hearings when the Liberals were in opposition. Crow, who was appointed and consistently defended by the Mulroney government, became something of a lightning rod in Canada for dissatisfaction over economic stagnation and high unemployment, but he was regarded as something of a hero by the management school graduates in red suspenders who have become the exemplars of the international financial system. This meant that getting rid of him could spark their ire, leading to a downgrading of Canada's debt and a rise in interest costs that could smother Martin's attack on the deficit before he had a chance to launch it.

Martin found a simple way out: He recommended to the prime minister that Crow not be reappointed but that his deputy, Gordon Thiessen, take his place. The more mild-mannered Thiessen was an orthodox inflation-fighter in the image of Crow, but he presented a more acceptable public face. Martin took a deep breath and waited to see how Wall Street would react. It didn't, which was good news for the rookie finance minister. He found himself with a central bank governor whose policies he understood — and which could no longer cause much additional harm. The new government benefited from a low-inflation environment. The policies that created this environment were politically unpopular and economically damaging, but it was the previous government and the outgoing bank governor who took the blame. The Liberals did not attempt to initiate any shift in monetary policy. With interest rates already dropping sharply, there was no need to do so. Inflation had turned into a non-issue by the time Paul Martin became finance minister, even if the Bank of Canada maintained its defensive ardour.

The deficit was a different story. Even the modest operating surpluses the Tories managed to achieve (which were offset many times over by payments on the public debt, especially after 1989 as John Crow's interest rate hikes bit hard) disappeared in the recession year of 1992 as revenues declined and spending requirements grew.

Much of the government's borrowing takes place outside Canada, and this confers an inordinate amount of power on foreign bond-rating agencies such as Moody's and Standard & Poor's. These agencies exist to help lenders determine whether borrowers are financially secure and how big a risk premium they will have to pay above the cheapest interest rates. If Moody's judges that a borrower is not being sufficiently orthodox in its fiscal policies, it can lower its rating by a notch or two, forcing the borrower to pay more in interest to its bondholders.

In the case of the government of Canada, which owes nearly $600 billion (as of 1998), simple arithmetic shows that just a half-point rise in average borrowing costs would mean an additional $3 billion per year — $100 for every person in Canada. That is money that would have to be taken from the pockets of taxpayers or squeezed out of public services, regardless of the social cost. And that does not even take account of the effects on provincial finances. Thus do supposedly sovereign governments become almost slavishly deferential to the potentates of Wall Street and their counterparts in London and Tokyo.

Obviously, there is a substantial price to pay for being part of the international financial system. But even if this were not the case — even if governments were not put under extortionate pressure by the men in red suspenders — the argument can be made that a fiscally healthy government is a stronger and nimbler government, with extra room to manoeuvre and more time to concern itself with the needs of the people who elected it.

Paul Martin, we will recall, was coauthor of the so-called Red Book, the policy booklet which the Liberals used so successfully in the 1993 election campaign and in which they pledged to bring the federal deficit to below 3 per cent of gross domestic product within three years. At a time when the deficit was running at close to 6 per cent of GDP, this seemed ambitious but not beyond reach. It was only since 1979 that the deficit had been running at more than 3 per cent. The 3 per cent figure had a nice ring to it, but it seemed to have been pulled out of thin air. It was the same figure that formed part of the Maastricht Treaty on European monetary union. Only countries whose governments run fiscal deficits below that magic number were deemed eligible to adopt the new joint European currency under the terms of the treaty.

In Canada, that figure is a bit misleading, since it takes account only of the federal deficit. Though several of the provinces were moving close to balanced budgets, Ontario and Quebec, which together account for well over 60 per cent of provincial spending, were still running big deficits. Critics from the Reform Party and other organizations of the political right complained that Martin's target was not ambitious enough. Few believed he would move close to a zero deficit in the Liberals' first term, and it was certainly not something that he pledged to pursue.

The early months of the Liberal government's tenure have been portrayed as a struggle for the soul of Paul Martin. According to Linda McQuaig in her book *The Cult of Impotence*, the combatants were the finance bureaucracy led by Deputy Minister David Dodge on one side and the junior finance minister, Doug Peters, on the other. Peters, a former chief economist with the Toronto-Dominion Bank who despite his establishment position was a critic of economic orthodoxy, argued for placing a higher priority on unemployment than on the deficit. For the officials — buttressed by Peter Nicholson, an influential adviser whom Martin brought in from the Bank of Nova Scotia in 1994 — deficit reduction was the only thing that mattered, and spending cuts were the only way to achieve it. After a long tug-of-war that lasted well past Martin's first budget in February 1994, Martin came around to the officials' view. According to McQuaig, the deciding factor was Martin's ambition: His hope for higher political office depended on maintaining the support of his business friends.

In their book *Double Vision*, Ottawa journalists Edward Greenspon and Anthony Wilson-Smith suggest different reasons for Martin's eventual embrace of a strong anti-deficit position. In their account, Peter Nicholson persuaded Martin that the deficit needed to be tackled before the problem of declining productivity could be addressed. In addition, Nicholson educated Martin about the inexorable effects of compound interest — as we have seen, Martin did not really need much education on that subject.

Undoubtedly, the role of two-fisted deficit fighter is not the only one Martin could have adopted. While he was not averse to downsizing in his years at Power Corporation and Canada Steamship Lines, he has at least as strong an inclination towards building as towards cutting, and he had been critical of Tory spending cuts in his speeches while in opposition and in the Red Book. The impetus for a frontal assault on the deficit clearly came from a single-minded finance department bureaucracy rather than from the minister himself. However, the idea of a struggle for Martin's soul is somewhat exaggerated. For another side of Martin is his ability to adjust his sights to fit the circumstances. His position as environment critic required him to become an enthusiastic environmentalist. Similarly, his position as finance minister required him to become a deficit cutter. There was a job to be done and he would do it.

The struggle-for-Martin's-soul scenario also overstates the extent to which there were real choices. "A party that was truly intent on following a different set of policies would have to be prepared to incur significant difficulties," says Manfred Bienefeld of Carleton University, a longtime observer and critic of Canadian economic policy. It would have been necessary to prepare people politically to withstand such eventualities as a lower bond rating, a run on the dollar, perhaps the withdrawal of some foreign investment. The Liberal Party — especially the Liberal Party of Jean Chrétien and Paul Martin — is hardly well suited to such a task. But in fairness, the Ontario NDP, which had to reverse course after introducing an expansionary deficit budget in 1990, was far from being up to the task either. Concentration on the deficit was the only realistic choice open to Martin in the circumstances with which he was presented, and the remaining questions were essentially ones of degree.

Deficit Wars

Elimination of the deficit came about in two simple and obvious ways: revenues grew, and spending fell. The elimination of certain loopholes such as the lifetime capital gains exemption helped on the revenue side. But fortunate timing played a much bigger part. With Canada moving briskly out of recession in 1994, federal revenues rose from not quite $116 billion in the 1993–94 fiscal year to nearly $141 billion just three years later. Economic growth meant that more people were working and paying taxes. A surging stock market and higher corporate profits brought higher revenues from the capital gains tax and corporate income tax. And a steady decline in interest rates meant that, by 1996, Canadian interest rates were lower than U.S. rates for the first time in recent memory.

All this resulted in the government moving back into an operating surplus in 1994–95 and to an overall surplus in 1997–98. The sharpest drop occurred between the 1995–96 fiscal year and 1996–97, when the federal deficit plunged from 3.6 per cent of gross domestic product to just 1.1 per cent. Martin also showed more political smarts than Michael Wilson in the way he presented deficit numbers. Instead of erring on the side of optimism and ending up looking silly, Martin took the opposite tack, consistently overestimating the size of the deficit. When the annual deficits came in at well below the forecast levels, he ended up looking good. He was even scolded in April 1998 by Auditor-General Denis Desautels, who accused him of making the figures look worse than they really were by incorporating spending for newly announced programs in the supplementary estimates a year or more before any disbursements actually occurred.

Martin's manipulation of deficit numbers is part of his political management of the budget process. This tactic has taken him into territory that none of his predecessors in the finance portfolio dared venture into. Martin makes decisions primarily on substance, but he also pays close attention to the way a measure can be communicated to the public. Indeed, he has occasionally failed to proceed with a measure he considered worthwhile because he could not be convinced that any effective way of communicating it could be found.

It wasn't so much that previous finance ministers did not believe in the value of communication. Rather, because of the tradition of budget secrecy, the notions of "budget" and "communication" were seen to belong in completely separate compartments. In 1963, even before controversy erupted over the contents of Walter Gordon's anti–foreign ownership budget, Gordon had to endure opposition attacks for having called in three outside consultants to work on budget preparation, in violation of the tradition that the budget should be known only to the finance minister and selected civil servants. Even as late as 1989, a leak that forced Michael Wilson to release his budget at a press conference instead of in the House of Commons led to angry accusations and criminal charges.

Martin has not completely abandoned the tradition of budget secrecy, but he has emptied it of most of its substance. Finance ministers began to conduct pre-budget consultations in the 1980s, and Martin has carried them to new levels. In the months leading up to each budget Martin speaks repeatedly about the broad themes he wishes to convey. Major budgetary items such as the Millennium Scholarship Fund have been announced separately before the budget. Other items have been leaked, without causing any of the controversy that used to erupt over budget leaks in the pre-Martin era.

Another element in Martin's communication package has involved the work of the Ottawa consulting firm Earnscliffe Strategy Group, two of whose principals, former CBC-TV Ottawa bureau chief Elly Alboim and former Young Liberals president David Herle, became integral members of Martin's team. Earnscliffe conducts extensive polling to assess how budget measures will be perceived. Alboim has also introduced Martin to devices and techniques he became familiar with at the CBC, such as Powerpoint, a sophisticated visual software system, and Perception Analyzer, which records the minute-by-minute reactions of citizens' panels to Martin's budget speeches.

Martin's emphasis on communications has paid off. If his achievement has been at least as much political as economic, the key element in his political success has been communication. Michael Wilson's spending cuts helped bring about the total destruction of the Tory government in 1993. Martin's no less far-reaching cuts did not prevent the Liberals from being reelected with a majority in 1997.

These spending cuts involved some heavy arm-twisting at the federal ministerial level as part of a process euphemistically called "program review." This was coupled with stark adjustments to federal–provincial shared-cost programs, producing the phenomenon that came to be known as downloading.

Greenspon and Wilson-Smith describe a series of private meetings starting in June 1994 involving individual cabinet ministers and their top officials. At these sessions, Martin, along with Intergovernmental Affairs Minister Marcel Massé (later named president of the treasury board), would set rigid targets for spending cuts in each department of government. A high-ranking finance department official, usually deputy minister David Dodge, would also attend these occasionally acrimonious conclaves. A different deputy minister, Harry Swain of the industry department, is reported to have denigrated these sessions, with their almost fundamentalist tone, as "Come-to-Jesus meetings."

> Invitations — some would say summonses — had been issued to each cabinet minister to drop by with their deputies and hear about something called program review. Martin, with Massé, his Cartesian other half, by his side, and a senior official, usually Dodge, sat down with each successive minister armed with little more than a small table of numbers, two lines over three years. The table laid out the current budgetary allocation for the department in question and the amount by which it was to be reduced in the 1995, 1996 and 1997 budgets under program review. The size of the required cuts left the ministers gasping; in many cases, they were well above 50 per cent.

Greenspon and Wilson-Smith recount the reactions of several ministers, among them Anne McLellan, then minister of natural resources, who later commented, "Right there, in the simple, deceptively simple, little piece of paper, they were going to destroy the Department of Natural Resources and remove any meaningful federal role in the resource sectors of this country." Sergio Marchi, then immigration minister, wondered if these figures had been conjured up by the same finance department officials who had served throughout the Tory reign. Were unelected officials issuing political judgements?

> Dodge had asked the same questions when Martin first assigned him to set the departmental targets. The deputy tried to fend him off, saying it was a political decision. Martin didn't have time to waste. He told his deputy that the politicians could work it out later. But he needed something to concentrate their minds right off the bat.

Grumble as they might, ministers and their deputies quickly learned that Martin had the full support of the prime minister. Perhaps no member of cabinet was hit harder by program review than Human Resources Minister Lloyd Axworthy, who had established his credentials as an advocate of activist government back in the Trudeau years. On the morning of October 5, 1994, the day he was to present to the House of Commons a major policy review that was already seriously watered down after months of discussions, Axworthy was floored by a newspaper headline revealing rumours of what turned out to be a treasury board estimate pointing to heavy social spending cuts in the coming years. A quick phone call to Martin from a top Axworthy aide failed to elicit a disavowal. Axworthy would in effect be proposing something that had already been squelched by financial constraints that went beyond what he anticipated.

This was not to be the last blow inflicted on him. Rather than achieving dreams of moving forward with a bold reform of social assistance policy that would modernize its focus and link it more closely with education and job training, Axworthy found himself presiding instead over the dismantling of the Canada Assistance Plan as it had existed since the era of Lester Pearson, along with Established Programs Financing, under which Ottawa paid 50 per cent of the costs of certain provincially administered programs such as health insurance. These programs were replaced with the Canada Health and Social Transfer, more commonly known as block funding, which left the provinces with smaller federal transfers but greater control over how this money could be spent. Axworthy, a freewheeling liberal in a cabinet run by by fiscal conservatives, found himself taking the public blame not only for a feared erosion of national standards in health care delivery but also for added restrictions on Unemployment Insurance and for cuts in support to postsecondary education.

For English-Canadian left nationalists, who have traditionally looked to the federal government for leadership in developing and maintaining Canada's welfare state, the Canada Health and Social Transfer represented Martin's worst affront. Maude Barlow and Bruce Campbell wrote that "it would roll back fifty years of federal leaderhip in creating the Canadian social state," and quoted the National Council on Welfare to the effect that "the proposed Canada Health and Social Transfer is the worst social policy initiative undertaken by the federal government in more than a generation." Others who were not so inclined to regard everything coming from Ottawa as good and everything coming from the provinces as bad had a different view. Former Liberal cabinet minister Eric Kierans wrote,

> The Canadian Health and Social Transfer is an expression of confidence that provinces can manage and improve the social security system now in place. The province is the arena where the deeply human realities of poverty, unemployment and declining opportunity have to be faced and defeated.

The Canada Health and Social Transfer and the reduction of transfer payments to the provinces have had and will have far-reaching implications (see chapter 5). Perhaps the safest statement that can be made about these changes is that the elimination of the federal deficit in five years would not have been possible without them.

Dominating the Agenda

In 1998, a federal surplus was a reality. The question then became: What should the government do with this surplus? It had several possibilities to choose from. It could start making a small dent in the almost $600-billion accumulated debt, it could start offering hard-pressed Canadians some tax relief, it could shift more money back into social spending to stitch up an increasingly tattered safety net, or it could do a little of each. At the time of writing, the direction that Martin and his colleagues were going to pursue was not at all clear.

Keynesian theory suggested that the government should wait until the economy really needed extra stimulus before offering tax relief or additional spending. Martin's own inclinations, again perhaps influenced by his personal experience with debt at Canada Steamship Lines, appeared to concur with those of Lord Keynes. Signs of this appeared in the spring of 1998, when Martin bested some of his cabinet colleagues yet again, at least initially, and the government took a hard line against blanket compensation for victims of tainted blood who had contracted hepatitis C. The Millennium Scholarship Fund was the only significant new spending item in the February 1998 federal budget, and it related to higher education, which is not even an area of federal jurisdiction. Martin had triumphed over the deficit but not over the debt, and he was not yet about to celebrate.

The elimination of the deficit came at a heavy cost. Hardly any part of Canada escaped hospital closings and other health service cuts as provincial governments coped both with their own deficit reduction targets and with the avalanche effect of federal downloading. Child care, one of the great remaining gaps in Canada's web of social programs, had scarcely been addressed. The universality of old-age pensions was eroded in a manner that Brian Mulroney would never have got away with (and would have been gutted further had Martin not suffered one of his rare defeats in cabinet). The much maligned Goods and Services Tax remained almost untouched (except in the

Atlantic region, where it was combined with sales taxes in three of the four provinces), despite an early commitment from Martin "to replacing the GST as soon as possible with a fairer, simpler system." Unemployment insurance premiums remained set at levels that far exceeded the requirements of the fund. And the list goes on.

Paul Martin's deficit elimination strategy dominated the agenda of the Chrétien government's first term in office and the early part of its second term in a way that has no parallel in federal politics since the war against Hitler and its immediate aftermath. Martin himself was only slightly less visible than the person who had defeated him in the 1990 Liberal leadership race. This is an obvious reflection on the magnitude of what he attempted and achieved, but it is also a sad comment on how little else the Chrétien government had set out to do. The Mulroney government has been widely vilified for its numerous and obvious shortcomings, but despite its Conservative label it was committed to change on many fronts. The free trade agreements, the Goods and Services Tax, and the Meech Lake constitutional agreement all had their flaws, but they represented initiatives of a government that was attempting to move the country in what it saw as a positive direction. In contrast, the Liberals under Jean Chrétien have given every indication of being firmly wedded to the status quo; it is the Liberals who have come across as the party of conservatism.

With the concentration on deficit reduction, Martin almost completely eclipsed the rest of the cabinet ministers during Chrétien's first term. Perhaps the only other minister who made a serious mark was Transport Minister Doug Young, who managed to tame the notoriously ferocious bureaucracy at the transport department by transferring operating units such as ports, airports and navigation systems to local authorities or autonomous bodies. By separating these units from the department's policy-making and inspection roles, Young ended a longstanding institutional conflict of interest. He was about to put his hand to reshaping the department of defence when voters in his New Brunswick riding put a brusque end to his political career in the 1997 general election.

There are many issues that Paul Martin has skirted or failed entirely to address in his public utterances as finance minister. There used to be standing jokes about the difficulty of finding the verbs in a Paul Martin, Sr., speech. It is just as difficult to find passages in Paul Martin, Jr., speeches that stray from the central themes of deficit reduction and fuzzy expressions of hope for the future. With the embarrassing exception of a speech in October 1995 during the Quebec referendum campaign in which he greatly exaggerated the extent of job losses in an independent Quebec, Martin's remarks have generally contained few surprises, proclaimed few new ideas and ruffled few feathers.

It seems only natural for him to dwell on the area where he has made his mark. His deficit fixation should not be taken as a sign that he is blind to other concerns, including human concerns that lie outside his direct ministerial ambit. In one of his first speeches as minister, delivered to management students in Montreal, he stated in remarks devoted mostly to the deficit that the government "will never be immune to the pain, the human tragedy that lies behind the numbers on the nation's balance sheet. The restoration of hope and the restoration of jobs must begin."

Critics would argue that it is difficult to reconcile such sentiments with Martin's subsequent actions and their effects on those who relied most heavily on government services. This does not, however, negate his record as the finance minister who has indisputably achieved more than anyone else who has held the portfolio in recent decades. He happened to be minister at a time in the country's history when matters of public finance had moved to centre stage, in a demonstrably conservative government in which activism and initiative were not strongly encouraged by the prime minister. He did what circumstances demanded, setting himself a task and using his talents to accomplish it. The way that task is perceived makes him an ogre

in some eyes and a saint in others. Martin has been called —
by the *Globe and Mail* — "the most successful finance minister
of the last 30 years." He has also been called — by former
Liberal cabinet member Paul Hellyer — "the worst finance
minister in memory." Hellyer and the *Globe* differ on whether
Paul Martin's program has been good or bad for the country,
but they are in agreement about the significance of that program and his effectiveness in carrying it out.

What if he had held a different post in cabinet? If he had
been human resources minister, for instance, would he have
fought as hard to maintain spending as he fought to curtail
spending in the post he actually held? And would he have
succeeded? There are many more what-ifs. What if he had
faced more resistance in cabinet, or from the provinces? What
if the prime minister had sided more often with other ministers?
What if the parliamentary opposition, or public opinion generally, had been less willing to accept spending cuts? Or does it
really matter now? The task ahead should be to identify areas
where the worst excesses have been committed and to set about
repairing the damage, whether it is Martin or someone else who
does it.

Martin family poses for a photographer after Martin Sr.'s re-election to Parliament in 1963. From left: Mary-Ann, Nell, Paul Sr., Paul Jr.

Paul Martin, Sr. and his followers campaign for the leadership of the Liberal Party in 1958. *Canapress Photo Service*.

Maurice Strong, one of Martin's mentors at Power Corporation, is shown here in 1966. *Canapress Photo Service.*

While he was at Power Corporation, Martin worked closely with Paul Desmarais, shown here in the 1980s. *Canapress Photo Service (Christopher Morris).*

Martin, president of the CSL Group, addresses the Canadian Council for Native Business in 1985. *The Gazette (Robert Lee).*

Martin, Liberal candidate in LaSalle-Émard, meets a striking employee of Voyageur Enterprises Ltd., a bus company owned by Martin's CSL Group, in 1988. *Canapress Photo Service (Allen McInnis).*

Martin celebrates his victory in 1988 in LaSalle-Émard with his wife Sheila and his father Paul Martin, Sr. *Canapress Photo Service (Shaney Komulainen).*

Martin speaks to reporters after announcing his candidacy for the leadership of the Liberal Party in 1990. *Canapress Photo Service (Ryan Remiorz).*

Martin and his wife Sheila campaign for the Liberal leadership in 1990. *The Gazette* (*John Mahoney*).

Finance Minister Martin tells reporters in 1993 that cutting spending isn't the only way to eliminate the deficit. *Canapress Photo Service (Fred Chartrand).*

Finance Minister Martin is congratulated by Prime Minister Chrétien after presenting a balanced budget on February 24, 1998. *Canapress Photo Service (Jonathan Hayward).*

Finance Minister Martin pauses to chat with Bank of Canada Deputy Governor Paul Jenkins (centre) and Governor Gordon Thiessen (right) in the spring of 1998. *Canapress Photo Service (Fred Chartrand).*

CHAPTER FIVE

A Dubious Legacy

If the task that Paul Martin accomplished had both political and economic dimensions, its consequences were also felt in both the political and economic spheres. Politically its consequences included a loss of twenty seats for the Liberals in the 1997 election in the Atlantic provinces, the region of the country that is poorest, most dependent on Ottawa and therefore hardest hit by Martin's spending cuts. Along with less drastic losses in the prairies, only partially offset by modest gains in Quebec, the rejection of the Liberals in the Atlantic region left them with a very narrow majority.

On the whole, however, the 1997 election had to be counted among Martin's successes. Given the magnitude of the spending cuts he had undertaken, what was remarkable was not that the Liberals lost seats but that they didn't lose more. In the key province of Ontario, they remained as dominant as they had been in 1993. With the opposition as badly divided as it had been in the previous parliament, the thin Liberal majority was not a cause for undue concern. Martin himself was easily reelected in LaSalle–Émard, and the $122,000 he received in campaign contributions was a reflection of business satisfaction with his performance in office in general and his attack on the deficit in particular. Two-thirds of the money donated to his campaign came from corporations — roughly double the level of corporate donations he had received in 1993. Another consequence of the taming of the deficit and the prominence of fiscal concerns in the Liberals' agenda was that Martin was by now widely regarded as the heir apparent to Chrétien.

Economically, the effects of the attack on the deficit were less straightforward and not widely felt in the short term. From the Trudeau era to Martin's time, proponents of deficit reduction have maintained that eliminating the deficit would restore confidence in the Canadian economy and promote stable economic growth. Thus, in October 1994 Martin characterized deficit reduction as "a precondition for sustained economic growth and job creation. Reduced deficits will in turn lead to lower interest rates, to higher consumer and business confidence and to the creation of new and lasting jobs." Has anything happened to bear out this contention? Martin's balanced budget of February 1998 was a famous victory, but what was actually gained by it? These questions can by explored by looking at a number of economic indicators: unemployment, the value of the Canadian dollar, savings rates and Martin's own personal fixation, productivity.

The Jobs Lag

All through the 1990s Canadian society has been wounded by unemployment rates that have risen and stayed four or five points above United States levels. For a time, jobless rates in Canada were stuck at over 11 per cent, and that was a country-wide average, masking rates above 20 per cent in some regions. Even after several years of economic growth, unemployment in 1998 was still above 8 per cent. In the United States, meanwhile, unemployment had fallen below 5 per cent and was still dropping, reaching a level of 4.3 per cent in April 1998 (compared to 8.4 per cent at the same time in Canada).

One particularly pernicious item of economic theory maintains that at the levels of unemployment prevailing in the United States in 1998, inflationary fires ought to be burning bright. The concept of the Non-Accelerating Inflationary Rate of Unemployment, with its equally charming abbreviation NAIRU, had taken hold in the 1970s as an offshoot of the monetarist teachings of the controversial Nobel Prize–winning economist Milton Friedman. The untested NAIRU theory, adopted by many economists and seemingly accepted as gospel at the Bank of Canada, suggests that there is a level of unemployment below which unacceptable inflationary pressures will build up. The growing body of polite skeptics has included Paul Martin, although he has been careful not to distance himself too obviously from the Bank of Canada.

Two big problems with NAIRU theory stand out. One is that there is no clear and accurate way of establishing where the NAIRU stands at a given time and place. At various times, Bank of Canada officials have suggested that Canada's NAIRU could be as high as 9 per cent. For a while, the benchmark level was 8 per cent. More recently, some adventurous souls in the NAIRU camp have conjectured that Canadian unemployment could fall as low as 7 per cent before the Bank of Canada has to start cranking up interest rates again. Another big problem with the NAIRU concept is that a growing body of evidence reveals it to be sheer nonsense. It is simply not being borne out by experience. Establishing a suitable NAIRU for the United States is no more an exact science than it is in Canada, but no NAIRU proponent would have suggested that unemployment could fall below 5 per cent without creating a fresh bout of price pressure. And yet no such pressure has manifested itself.

There are many factors to explain why unemployment should be higher in Canada than in the United States. First, there is the old bugaboo about harsher winters leading to a higher proportion of seasonal jobs, with the working season often very much shorter in Canada. Nowadays, with a smaller part of the Canadian workforce engaged in farming and other sectors affected by big seasonal variations, this explanation has been wearing ever thinner.

Canada's more generous social assistance programs, coupled with a stronger union movement and a lower propensity to leave home in search of work, all point to less flexible labour markets, if you accept current economic jargon, or to a lower level of desperation on the part of the unemployed, in real human terms. The net results are both bad and good: They do indicate lost economic opportunity in Canada, with all that this implies in terms of lower living standards, especially for the jobless, but it also means that Canadians are spared some of the insecurity that Americans experience, including a widespread fear that job loss may also bring a loss of proper medical coverage.

Finally, Canada's relatively high immigration levels are sometimes suggested as a cause of higher unemployment. (Legal immigration has run at about three times U.S. rates on a per-capita basis, with total levels still probably more than double even after illegal entry is taken into account.) This notion appears to be based mostly on ignorance and prejudice. Immigrants create jobs as well as taking jobs, they often perform jobs that people born in Canada are less able or willing to do, and they generally show an exemplary eagerness to work.

Some of the above are valid explanations of Canada's higher-than-U.S. unemployment rates, and some are not. But all of them applied in previous decades, when the gap between Canadian and U.S. unemployment rates was much narrower. Even if the gap is not as wide as it appears (for instance, the large U.S. prison population is not, by definition, available for work, adding a few tenths of a point to the true unemployment rate), the fact remains that the gap has held at far broader levels in the 1990s than before. Some factors help explain why the "natural" unemployment rate in Canada should be a point or two higher than in the United States, but they come nowhere close to explaining a gap of four or five points.

While the U.S. Federal Reserve Board, like the Bank of Canada, sought to trim inflation, it was more subtle in its approach than its Canadian counterpart. The Fed, under Alan Greenspan, appeared quite willing to accept annual inflation rates running a point to a point and a half higher than those that prevailed in Canada through most of the 1990s. Indeed, there is no ironclad rule in economics stating that inflation has to be near zero, and in many circles a little inflation is considered a small price to pay for extra job-creating growth. It almost seemed as if the Fed, in contrast to the Bank of Canada, actually put the people and the communities economic policy is meant to serve ahead of abstract anti-inflation theories.

And just who are these people and communities? While some of Greenspan's immediate crowd has indeed been drawn from among the wealthy few for whom investment income is more important than employment or pension income, it has recently dawned on many of these same people that something approaching full employment is not necessarily inimical to their interests. In the years immediately following the recession of the early 1990s, reports of lower unemployment would almost invariably send share prices on Wall Street into a tail-spin because of inflation fears, but once the flaws in NAIRU and associated theories became more evident, employment figures and share prices began to move almost in lockstep rather than in opposite directions. It is no mystery that higher employment means higher sales and higher profits.

With Canada finally emerging in the middle 1990s from job-destroying restrictions on the money supply, the same virtuous cycle began to take hold here. Indeed, Chrétien, Martin and other Canadian politicians were able to boast at international gatherings about how solid the fundamentals of the Canadian economy had become, with healthy growth, negligible inflation, a healthy trade surplus and a growing federal budget surplus. But the indicator through which most people actually benefit from a healthy economy — jobs — still lagged behind, representing lost opportunity and human distress on a massive scale.

The Falling Dollar

Nor did all the good news prevent the Canadian dollar from falling to record lows against the U.S. dollar, with closing levels barely above 63 cents in September 1998 and, who knows, maybe lower still since these words were written.

There are several possible explanations for the slide in the value of the Canadian dollar, the chief among them being that nominal interest rates on Canadian bonds had gone below U.S. rates and were barely any higher than U.S. rates even when adjusted for inflation. Thus, to many investors around the globe, U.S. securities had become more attractive, particularly in the light of the severe financial problems that erupted in eastern Asia in 1997, leading not only to lower prices and volumes for Canadian commodity exports but also to market jitters that steered investment to the safest of havens — the United States. As well, Canadian government requirements for fresh borrowing had dried up, further reducing foreign demand for Canadian dollars. With neither deficits nor inflation exerting upward pressure on Canadian interest rates in 1998, it appeared that returns on Canadian bonds would remain relatively low, holding demand for the loonie at modest levels.

Even as the sliding dollar became front-page news in the summer of 1998, both Chrétien and Martin remained publicly unconcerned. Thus on August 6, after the dollar had closed down at 65.385 cents, Martin maintained that he and the government were "not indifferent to the behaviour of the currency," but he emphasized the strengths of the Canadian economy: "If you take a look at where we were in terms of debt, deficit, rising taxes, inflation and compare where the Canadian economy has come over the last number of years, you understand Canadians have won a great victory."

The Bank of Canada, in whose purview this matter clearly lies, also did not seem unduly concerned, although it did intervene in the money markets to keep the dollar above 65 cents the day after Martin made his remarks. Meanwhile, a debate erupted over the wisdom of this official insouciance, although few went so far as to suggest that the Bank of Canada should raise interest rates — a standard remedy for a beleaguered currency but one that could have deleterious effects on a still fragile Canadian economy. Some saw the dollar's slide as a reflection of underlying economic weakness; others maintained that it was entirely caused by extraneous events. In any case, it was hardly the vote of confidence that Paul Martin wanted in the wake of his February balanced budget announcement.

The Productivity Puzzle

One question that does appear to evoke Martin's concern, although this has been more evident in private conversations than in public comments, is Canada's poor productivity performance in the 1990s. Indeed, the need to do something about productivity was one of the clinching arguments that persuaded Martin to undertake an all-out assault on the deficit in 1994. Peter Nicholson, whom Martin brought in from the Bank of Nova Scotia as a special adviser, forcefully argued that productivity was the key to economic growth and that Canada's ongoing productivity problems could not be addressed unless the deficit was brought under control. While Martin was initially resistant to this message, by October 1994 he had made it his own:

> Better productivity is not the enemy of employment; it is our workers' best friend. How do we improve productivity? To my mind and to all of our minds, the answer is clear. We must improve our skills. We must do better at innovation. We must provide a welcoming climate for investment. We must remove the disincentives we have created for both business and individuals — disincentives that encourage dependence and stand in the way of opportunity. Finally we must get our fiscal house in order.

Productivity can be measured by subtracting employment growth from the rise in gross domestic product. For example, if GDP rises 3.5 per cent in a given year and the number of people employed in producing this output grows by 2 per cent, then productivity has risen by 1.5 per cent. Higher productivity, by definition, means fewer workers are required to produce the same quantity of goods. To some proponents of full employment, it does not bring unmitigated benefits, and it was this double-edged effect that made Martin hestiate before embracing the productivity argument advanced by Nicholson. But it is precisely this ability to produce more with less labour that enables people living in advanced economies to benefit from high living standards.

Since the middle 1980s, Canada's rate of productivity growth has lagged below that of the United States and well below that of previous decades. This occurred despite the corporate downsizings of the early 1990s (and the government downsizings that followed soon afterward) that were intended precisely to raise productivity. A 1994 Statistics Canada study found that business productivity in Canada and the United States had risen by roughly comparable amounts since 1961, with Canadian productivity growth higher on average during the first two and a half decades of this period but lagging after 1985. This same study found that, partly as a result, Canadian unit labour costs (wages and benefits per unit of production) rose between 1986 and 1991 when measured in U.S. dollars, though this also had much to do with the high value of the Canadian dollar during part of this period. Starting in 1992, Canadian unit labour costs began falling again, partly because of the declining dollar and partly also because of an above-average productivity rise in 1994. This contributed to a surge in exports to the United States. But at least as important an explanation was stagnant wages in Canada. As the Statistics Canada study noted, 1994 saw "the second consecutive decrease in unit labour costs for the Canadian business sector, a result not seen in 48 years."

Productivity growth goes hand in hand with the value of the dollar in determining Canada's competitive position on a world scale. But a lower dollar can provide only temporary relief from the problems created by lagging productivity rises. Except for deficit reduction, not much progress has been made in the other areas Martin identified as essential for boosting productivity, indicating that the answers may not be as clear as he suggested.

The Millennium Scholarship Fund announced in the 1998 budget aimed to make postsecondary education more broadly accessible. Better educated workers tend to be more productive workers, and despite high jobless rates, employers complain of difficulties in finding qualified applicants for certain job openings. Education can help, but it is not a panacea. It is often assumed that most unemployed people are unable to find jobs because they lack the skills needed in a modern economy. Despite an undeniable mismatch between available workers and vacant jobs, it bears repeating that diplomas do not guarantee jobs. Many readers will have heard tales of doctoral graduates driving taxis. Although true examples may be rather rare, less extreme cases of underemployment are quite common. (The market supposedly sees to it that wage levels reflect the relative scarcity of qualified applicants. The job category with the sharpest rise in remuneration in the 1990s has been that of chief executive officer. Obviously, the market has been signalling that there is a serious shortage of corporate CEOs.)

One of the more coherent economic arguments in support of the original 1988 Canada–U.S. Free Trade Agreement and of subsequent trade deals held that forcing Canadian industry to compete on equal terms in a much bigger market would create a major thrust towards productivity growth. Although some industrial sectors have indeed shown dramatic improvements, others have stagnated, leaving many economists baffled. Productivity growth in the Canadian economy averaged less than 1 per cent a year in the early and middle 1990s even after taking account of a relatively strong 1.9 per cent rise in 1997, which in turn may have resulted in part from a surge of machinery imports that year and the previous year. The average since 1989 has been significantly lower than in the United States. In fact, it has been significantly worse than in any decade since the 1930s.

Despite these poor numbers and the declining competitiveness they signal, Canadian exports were going gangbusters, especially to the United States, whose share of Canadian export sales had risen to more than 80 per cent. (Since exports make up more than 40 per cent of Canadian production, sales to the United States account for about one-third of everything made in Canada.) Canadian industrialists evidently have seen little need to spend money on expensive equipment or training with wage levels showing scarcely any rises. Aided by lower-than-U.S. inflation rates and a sliding Canadian dollar, their competitive edge was rising automatically by about 2 per cent a year without their having to lift a finger.

Poor productivity growth will ultimately mean that Canadian living standards will continue to stagnate or decline. Figures drawn from the 1996 census show that average family incomes, when adjusted for inflation, had not recovered to the levels of the late 1980s and in fact were close to where they had been in the 1981 census. Even if there has been some slow improvement since 1996, the devastating effects of the recession still linger.

The Savings Decline

Another less noticed effect of the lingering hardships affecting many Canadians has been a dramatic decline in personal savings rates. Canadians were long among the top savers in the western world, but the 1990s have produced a sizeable reversal. Canada now ranks near the bottom as people try to maintain or improve their living standards on paycheques that have scarcely risen in value. Much of what Canada gained through elimination of government deficits has thus been offset by massive dissaving at the personal level. Even some upper-middle-class Canadians are taking the capital gains on their investments and simply spending them instead of reinvesting. (Some economists point out that pension funds and stock portfolios account for a larger share of personal assets than in the past. This makes total personal savings harder to measure, and the decline in savings rates may be less than it appears. It also means savings levels may be more volatile as stock prices fluctuate.)

Martin's 1998 Budget Plan predicted that savings would start rebounding towards normal levels as household incomes rose, but this was pure conjecture. There seems little that government can do to change the recent trend towards dissaving. The tax system already provides generous treatment for RRSPs and related schemes. The greatest benefit, of course, goes to those who are already in a position to save. (To nobody's surprise, Statistics Canada has reported that taxpayers with higher incomes are likelier to make annual RRSP contributions than people of more modest means.) The only other possibilities would be mandatory savings plans or sharply higher Canada Pension Plan contributions. Neither of these ideas is much of a vote-winner.

All told, the economic benefits of Paul Martin's successful attack on the deficit have been somewhere between inconclusive and modest. But perhaps the most far-reaching effects have been felt in an area where politics and economics meet: the balance between the federal government and the provinces.

Nowhere were these implications as keenly felt as in Ontario, which elected a rambunctiously ideological Conservative government within months of Martin's landmark 1995 budget. Unlike the federal Liberals, whose focus on the deficit ruled out tax reduction as well as social spending, Mike Harris's Ontario Tories cut income taxes by 30 per cent while the province was still running a deficit, recalling Ronald Reagan's supply-side tax cuts of the 1980s. The interplay between Paul Martin and the Ontario Tories is one of the more revealing aspects of the way in which the politics and economics of deficit reduction have played out.

Devolution and Globalism

In a column describing provincial reaction to Paul Martin's February 1998 budget, Toronto *Star* columnist Richard Gwyn dismissed the premiers' complaints as "sparring ... just another round in the endless federal-provincial battle." The essence of the budget, he wrote, was that the "national government is re-emerging as a political power."

Gwyn went on to describe succinctly the hollowing out of the federal government over the past period and how Canada had become by far the most decentralized country in the industrialized world. Now, however, things were apparently going to change. He cited the announced Millennium Scholarship Fund, which demonstrated "that Ottawa is once again activist, assertive, and — as Chrétien and Martin showed — is now entirely unapologetic about being so."

The issue is not whether the feds want to revitalize federal power — indeed they may actually want to — but whether they can. In a vacuum, one might suggest that having downloaded and cut transfer payments to reduce the federal deficit, the government could at some point upload and move back into areas such as health and a grateful country would welcome it back. However, the federal cuts in transfer payments are part of a larger process. Thus, Premier Harris noted that when his predecessor Bob Rae, in the last months of his mandate, protested the original cuts in transfer payments and especially their unfairness to Ontario, "I didn't whine." Indeed he didn't. Instead, once in power, he moved both to download the cuts onto the municipalities and to order even steeper cuts.

Expressing concern that the federal government will now attempt to move directly into areas of provincial jurisdiction with its apparent surplus, Saskatchewan's Roy Romanow, certainly the most experienced politician in the area of federal–provincial relations as well as premier of a "have-not" province and thus by definition a defender of federal authority, acknowledged that the federal government has the right to deal directly with Canadians without working through the provinces. However, he added, this general concept needs to be defined to limit the ability of Ottawa to spend for strictly political purposes. The suggestion that Ottawa be restricted in its general dealings with the public, coming from a presumably staunch federalist such as Romanow who leads a province that is a traditional beneficiary of federal monies, indicates how far the devolution of federal authority has gone since Martin becan his deficit-cutting exercise.

The federal government now finances only 40 per cent of government program costs in Canada. The provinces are responsible for 60 per cent. In this connection, the provinces that cover most of the federal cost are Ontario and Alberta, neither of which is governed by politicians who are overly enthusiastic supporters of social welfare programs, even in their own provinces. As the federal role declines, either the slack is taken up by the provincial government on which these costs have been downloaded — for which the Ontario NDP government paid with its life — or the slack is left slack.

In most cases, the provincial governments have merely cut back and downloaded themselves. On the one hand, economic growth has produced substantial increases in government income. In Ontario, the 1998 deficit is about $1.4 billion lower than projected, as revenue increases have more than offset a 3 per cent rise in government expenditures. (Ontario still has a deficit and hence its accumulated debt is still rising, but this is due to Harris's tax cuts.) But with all this money filling government coffers, health, education and social welfare programs in Ontario and elsewhere, developed decades ago in a much smaller and weaker economy, are in ruins.

Responding to Premier Harris's criticism of the last federal budget, Martin said that while Ontario lost $850 million in federal health and education funding, it had lost $4.8 billion because of its tax cuts. Jean Chrétien chimed in, "Mr. Harris? What did he do? Rather than balance the books he decided to cut taxes. So now he has a problem balancing the books. So he blames the government."

These answers to Harris are irrelevant. It is quite true that the Harris tax cuts are indefensible in the context of the crisis in social service spending — created mainly by the last few federal budgets — and that Ontario could afford to take up the slack. But it is also beside the point. As Harris noted on several occasions, the booming Ontario economy was a decisive factor in the massive increase in federal revenues that enabled the deficit to be eliminated. Moreover, the cutbacks in federal transfers hurt Ontario more than the other provinces. Ontario was "shortchanged" by billions of dollars then. "I didn't whine then," Harris said, "but now that you [Ottawa] are in surplus, largely on the back of Ontarians, then I think it's fair to point that out."

But what about the provinces that couldn't take up the slack? Toronto *Star* columnist Tom Walkom gives some perspective relating the 1998 provincial election in Nova Scotia (in which the NDP won as many seats as the governing Liberals) to a new Canadian economic reality. "There seems to be a more fundamental transformation taking place along the East Coast," he wrote, "one which is bringing the political system into alignment with the post-NAFTA economic world." Walkom related the previous domination of Atlantic politics by the Liberals and Conservatives to the region's dependence on Ottawa. However, the redefinition of the Canadian economy through Brian Mulroney's free trade deals and the realignment of government finances under Jean Chrétien destroyed the old patterns:

Ottawa's fiscal stinginess was not simply the result of tough times, it was a sign that the old Canada no longer existed, and that the old parties were no longer interested. … In the post-NAFTA world, the central government has become largely illusory. Why then bother supporting the parties which traditionally have controlled the government?

All of which proves once again that we don't live in a vacuum. In addition to Canada's internal reality, there is the new reality created by the external, invisible and yet ever-present force called globalism.

Enter Thomas J. Courchene. Courchene is an outspoken and prominent constitutional expert. He is also a Conservative and an admirer of Mike Harris's Common Sense Revolution with the caveat that he distances himself from the Ontario government's crude, ham-fisted approach to most of the reforms he considers needed, indeed overdue. With that said, Courchene, along with doctoral candidate Colin R. Telmer (who according to his biographical note is in transit to Finance Canada), published 1n 1998 a 311-page "interpretive essay" entitled *From Heartland to North American Region State: The Social, Fiscal and Federal Evolution of Ontario*.

As characterized by *Globe and Mail* reviewer John Barber, "The book argues persuasively that Ontario has changed overnight from the unnoticeable heartland of a peaceable kingdom into one of the most functionally autonomous, economically distinctive subnational jusisdictions in the world." Overnight in Barber's eyes is a decade. Let's see: 1998 back to 1988, the year of the free trade election.

Essentially, Courchene and Telmer describe the systematic devolution of political power from the federal government to the provinces. Power may be the wrong word to apply to most of Canada's provinces, but it fits exactly with Ontario's position. With free trade, Ontario went through a painful economic transition from the industrial heartland envisaged in John A. Macdonald's National Policy to a north–south economic (and increasingly political) relationship. They also lay out the political implications of the fact that, with the exception of Quebec, Ontario simply does not do much business with Canada any more.

Thus, prairie farmers used to complain about paying a premium on tariff-protected agricultural equipment shipped at high rates from Ontario instead of being able to buy equipment from the American midwest. Well, Ontario doesn't make any agricultural equipment any more. Meanwhile, Ontario's automobile assembly and parts manufacturing have expanded greatly, and now represent an $80-billion-a-year industry. This industry is based almost totally on export. Canada, east and west, now shops and buys its goods where they are the cheapest. Ontario's disengagement from the rest of Canada applies in a trade sense now, and it will increasingly apply in a political sense as Ontario begins to balk at equalization payments, starts its own income tax system and demands prior consultation and consent on international economic and financial agreements.

Another interesting aspect of the reforms ushered in by the Harris government in Ontario is that at their base both the Liberals and NDP agree with them. Education reform, market value assessment, health care restructuring and reforming urban governance, all key elements of the Harris agenda, were part of the NDP's program in office, and some of these initiatives like education reform and health care restructuring were already underway. There is also scant difference between Liberal and Conservative budgetary philosophies, at least as they work themselves out in practice. Or to put it another way, the difference in practice between Paul Martin and Ontario Treasurer Ernie Eves is no greater than that between Martin's federal budgets from 1995 on and the Liberals' 1993 Red Book.

Paul Martin is far from being an ideological foe of activist government, and he argues that the market cannot be left completely to itself. Yet his environment militates against these wishes. Martin did not initiate a process: He has merely presided over one. If he wishes to reassert federal power, he will have to attempt to reverse the process of devolution much more firmly than with a Millennium Scholarship Fund — if any reversal is possible or even appropriate at this time.

CHAPTER SIX

Balancing Act

Early 1998 seemed, in many ways, the best of times for Paul Martin. With his February 24 budget he brought his four-year campaign to eliminate the deficit to a successful conclusion, turning a trick that no other finance minister had managed in almost three decades. His status as the most powerful minister in the Chrétien cabinet was beyond contention — indeed, he exercised more power than any other cabinet minister since C.D. Howe in the 1950s. Less exalted ministers competed for his favour, and carefully factored his apprehended approval into the programs they brought forward to cabinet.

In the Ottawa fishbowl, events were increasingly being interpreted in the light of a possible upcoming Liberal leadership campaign, even though the prime minister's office was occupied by a highly popular politician who was visibly enjoying his job. And in this perspective the undoubted front-runner was Paul Martin, who was increasingly referred to as the heir apparent or *le dauphin*. Martin helped fuel the speculation by behaving like a politician who was running for something. On an August Sunday afternoon he showed up at a corn roast near Stratford, Ontario, posing for pictures and explaining his presence only by saying that he was originally from southwestern

Ontario and welcomed the opportunity to return to the area and meet with people like host Brian Innes and his family.

While Martin bore the political scars of the fight against the deficit, the aura of the "successful businessman with a social conscience" with which he had entered politics had never completely left him. He towered above the other Liberals generally mentioned as possible candidates: Allan Rock, Anne McLellan, Brian Tobin — especially after Rock's leadership aspirations were severely damaged by the controversy over compensation of hepatitis C sufferers, which was largely fuelled by the Liberals' adherence to Martin's notions of fiscal prudence.

Furthermore, as an Anglo-Quebecer of Franco-Ontarian origin, Martin shares and exploits the cultural ambiguity that has been almost a condition of survival for recent Canadian prime ministers: Pierre Elliott Trudeau, the product of a mixed French-Scottish marriage; Brian Mulroney, the working-class Irish Catholic raised in a predominantly francophone industrial town; Jean Chrétien, who although thoroughly French Canadian in his roots has spent a political lifetime building bridges to English Canada, to the point where as prime minister he has established a much stronger base in English Canada than in Quebec.

As a result of his support for the Meech Lake Accord during the 1990 leadership campaign, Martin also has a reputation as less of a hard-line foe of Quebec nationalism than Chrétien, which could position him to win back some of the Liberals' historic Quebec support that since 1984 has gone first to the Conservatives and then to the Bloc Québécois. Indeed, some observers see Martin as a leader who could reverse the slow contraction of the Liberals' base that has been the long-term trend since the 1950s. Under King and Saint-Laurent the Liberals were a genuine Canada-wide coalition; in 1949 they won a majority of seats in every province except Alberta. The Pearson-Trudeau Liberals were more of a Quebec-Ontario coalition, with only scattered and sporadic representation in the Atlantic provinces and the west. Under Chrétien the Liberals' base has largely been reduced to the single province of Ontario, which has kept them in power by practising bloc voting on a scale unmatched even in Trudeau-era Quebec. If Martin could appeal to the west through fiscal conservatism as well as to Quebec through flexible federalism, he could be the leader who would finally turn things around and begin to broaden their base again.

Given all these assets on his side, it would be tempting to suggest that all Martin needs to do is pick up the keys to 24 Sussex Drive. And there is little doubt that if the Liberal leadership were to become open in the immediate future, Martin would be virtually unstoppable. It is far more likely, however, that Chrétien will stick around until, say, late 2000 or early 2001. At that point, Martin will be sixty-two, and no Liberal since Louis Saint-Laurent has assumed the party leadership at such an advanced age (indeed, in recent decades only David Lewis, who was sixty-two when he became NDP leader in 1971, has assumed the leadership of any major party past the age of sixty). Nor is it only a question of age. If the Liberals seek to veer back towards greater emphasis on social programs, as they seemed to be preparing to do at their 1998 annual convention, they are unlikely to choose the hero of the war on the deficit as their champion.

Rather, they could easily be tempted to fall back on the Liberal tradition of choosing a leader unsullied by the recent past. As we have seen, as Lester Pearson's leadership limped towards its conclusion in 1967, Paul Martin, Sr., was widely regarded as the front-runner in the race to succeed him, and no one foresaw the sudden rise of the rookie MP from Mount Royal, Pierre Elliott Trudeau. In early 1998, a potential candidate of this sort was already being talked about. Jane Stewart, the minister of Indian affairs and northern development, was still in her early forties, had won the respect of the officials in her department, and — as the granddaughter of Ontario Premier Harry Nixon and daughter of Provincial Treasurer Bob Nixon — had a Liberal pedigree to rival Paul Martin's. As happened with his father, Martin might wait for his time to come only to find that it has already passed.

The Conflict of Interest Pitfall

One thing was clear. If Martin were to make it to the top, he would need to keep his balance on the tightrope between business and politics that had characterized his career. And in the weeks before his triumphal 1998 budget, there was an incident suggesting that this balance was a little shaky.

The incident arose in connection with Bill C-28, an omnibus bill sponsored by the minister of finance that covered 468 pages, had 301 separate provisions, and sought to amend the Income Tax Act and at least seventeen other pieces of fiscal legislation. Now omnibus bills are dubious democratic devices at the best of times. It is unlikely that most members who vote on such bills are aware of the implications of more than a small part of what they were voting on. Even the minister presenting an omnibus bill may not be aware of everything that is in it. Indeed, as Bill C- 28 became controversial, Paul Martin's lack of awareness of one of its clauses would be an important point in his defence.

The clause in question, number 241, was an amendment to paragraphs 250(6)(a) and (b) of the Income Tax Act, which deal with the tax treatment of shipping companies. It occurred to some opposition MPs, and especially to Yvan Loubier, the member for Saint-Hyacinthe–Bagot and finance critic for the Bloc Québécois, that this clause might benefit the CSL Group, owned by Paul Martin.

When someone with business interests as extensive as Martin's occupies a portfolio with as broad-ranging an impact on the economy as finance, it is virtually inevitable that the possibility, suggestion or appearance of conflict of interest will arise at some point. For instance, before his election to Parliament, Paul Martin held directorships on the boards of several large firms, including the Manufacturers Life Insurance Company. With him as minister, life insurance companies successfully lobbied the department of finance to defer changes to the Bank Act that would have authorized Canada's banks to sell insurance products in their branches, thereby offering consumers the benefit of greater competition. Martin also sat on the board of Imasco, a diversified holding company whose subsidiaries include Imperial Tobacco, which dominates the Canadian cigarette market. Soon after Martin became finance minister, the government had to confront the problem of large-scale cigarette smuggling into eastern Canada, a situation made possible by the tobacco companies' practice of shipping large quantities of cigarettes to the smugglers' U.S.-based suppliers. At cabinet behest, the finance department caved in, dramatically lowering the excise tax on cigarettes. This cut the ground out from under the smugglers but at the same time rewarded Imperial Tobacco and its sister companies with lower retail prices for their products, helping them gain an even larger flow of new teenaged addicts. And in his takeover of Canada Steamship Lines, Martin had received hefty loans from the Royal Bank of Canada, which in 1998 was demanding government approval of its proposed merger with the Bank of Montreal.

Another incident involved the sale of the Toronto textbook firm Ginn Publishing Canada by a federal crown corporation, the Canada Development Investment Corporation, to its original owner, the American media conglomerate Paramount Communications. The circumstances of the sale were murky and the affair erupted in the House of Commons in March 1994, with the opposition Bloc Québécois assuming the mantle of defender of Canadian cultural sovereignty.

In an article in *Maclean's* a month later, Marci McDonald noted that Paul Martin, whose department was responsible for the CDIC, had business dealings with a Paramount subsidiary, the Famous Players movie theatre chain. Through a family holding company, Nellmart Ltd., Martin was part owner of three Vancouver movie theatres that were leased to Famous Players. This arrangement was a legacy of the association between longtime Famous Players head Paul Nathanson and Paul

Martin, Sr., who in 1957 had acquired an interest in the theatres which he eventually passed on to his son. Was Martin's association with Paramount close enough to make it improper for him to be involved in decisions surrounding the Ginn sale? The government's Ethics Counsellor, Howard Wilson, thought not: "He's in a landlord relationship with Famous Players, not an investment relationship." McDonald reported in *Maclean's* that Martin had met with Industry Minister John Manley and Heritage Minister Michel Dupuy to discuss the sale, but when questioned in the House of Commons Manley denied that any such meeting had taken place.

We are not suggesting here that Paul Martin's earlier corporate directorships or holdings influenced government decisions or that there was any violation of conflict of interest guidelines. But instances such as these, where the public interest was served in questionable fashion, show how difficult it can be to avoid the *appearance* of conflict of interest. As far back as 1983, Martin had met privately with a task force co-chaired by Mitchell Sharp and Michael Starr, former Liberal and Tory cabinet ministers respectively, that was studying the whole question of conflict of interest. As Sharp described it, "He sought advice on conflict of interest rules that would govern the handling of his business interests if he decided to seek office."

When Martin became minister of finance in 1993, his interest in Passage Holdings Inc., through which he owns the CSL Group and Canada Steamship Lines, was placed in a blind management agreement, the type of divestment recommended by the office of the government's Ethics Counsellor for assets of this sort. A blind management agreement differs from a blind trust, where the trustee can buy and sell securities on the owner's behalf so that the owner does not know exactly what his or her holdings are. Paul Martin is perfectly well aware that he is the owner of Canada Steamship Lines, and he is kept informed of the company's performance. But he is not at all involved in the management of the corporation.

This still leaves open the possibility that, as minister of finance, he may be directly involved in decisions that would affect Canada Steamship Lines. In fact, there are many such decisions, but most of these would affect CSL as one of a broad range of corporations, and participating in decisions of this nature is not considered a conflict of interest. However, as Ethics Counsellor Howard Wilson told the Commons Finance Committee on February 17, 1998,

> There are some other areas, however, where decisions would have a very specific and direct impact on his private interests. This would be the case regarding ship-building policy or decisions regarding the subsidization of Via Rail, because of his interest in Voyageur. Mr. Martin decided that he should not participate on these issues and has therefore delegated responsibility to his Secretary of State, initially the Honourable Doug Peters and now the Honourable James Peterson, for shipbuilding, marine transportation, Via and the St. Lawrence Seaway.

This was the procedure followed in the case of clause 241 of Bill C-28. Jim Peterson, the secretary of state for international financial institutions, took responsibility for this clause, although Martin was still the sponsor of the bill as a whole. So if Martin was not in a conflict of interest, he was in the rather odd position of presenting legislation to the Commons for which he was not responsible.

As the controversy progressed, a number of versions were floated as to exactly what the effect of clause 241 would be on shipping companies in general and the CSL Group in particular. The most credible version emerged in the course of an exchange between Yvan Loubier and the director general of the Department of Finance's tax legislation division, Leonard Farber, in the Commons Finance Committee on February 10. According to Farber, the purpose of the clause was to make it more attractive for foreign shipping companies to locate their headquarters in Canada by making the income of these companies' foreign subsidiaries exempt from taxation. The legislation, he said, merely formalized a longstanding administrative procedure that was standard practice not only in Canada but also in most other industrialized countries. Moreover, clause 241 represented only "minor technical amendments" to a provision that had been in force since 1991.

Under questioning from Loubier, Farber acknowledged that the foreign shipping companies envisioned in the clause could include the foreign subsidiaries of Canadian-owned companies:

> If the question relates to the possibility of a structure that has a Canadian parent company incorporated and resident in Canada, and has a host of subsidiaries, or a subsidiary, incorporated in a foreign country, and that subsidiary is carrying on the business under the conditions I indicated to you, and that subsidiary, or the parent of that company, chooses to repatriate the management of that company to Canada and operate that subsidiary out of Canada, then yes, these provisions could be available to that company.

Farber also made it clear that the provisions applied only to shipping companies and not to companies operating in any other industry.

The specific technical amendment introduced in clause 241 involves a situation where the foreign subsidiary in question (call it "A") does not operate ships on its own account, but is itself the parent company of further subsidiaries ("B", "C" and "D") that actually operate the ships. In this case, subsidiary A would be treated as if it operated the ships sailing under the umbrella of subsidiaries B, C and D, and would benefit from the tax break in the legislation. One company with such a structure is the CSL Group, which has a wholly owned subsidiary called CSL Self Unloader Investment Ltd. Bermuda, which in turn owns additional subsidiaries in Barbados and Liberia.

Why would a company structure itself in this way? According to a background paper issued by the Bloc Québécois, "First of all because this makes it possible to register each of its ships in the country of its choice and thus benefit from the advantages that each of these countries offers." The countries in question are tax havens such as Bermuda, Barbados and Liberia. In addition, and even more important, "it is in a company's interest to structure itself in this way to limit its responsibilities." Thus, if a ship owned by subsidiary D were involved in a major spill of toxic materials, the liability would be limited to subsidiary D. Even if this subsidiary were forced to declare bankruptcy, subsidiaries B and C, and the profits flowing from them to subsidiary A, would not be affected.

Ethics Counsellor Wilson investigated the allegations of conflict of interest and reported to the Commons Finance Committee on February 17 that they were baseless. Wilson had spoken to CSL officials, who had told him that the company would not benefit from clause 241:

I spoke early on February 3rd to Mr. Stuart Hyndman, one of the supervisors of Mr. Martin's blind management agreement, as well as to Mr. Pierre Préfontaine, vice-president and counsel for CSL. I wanted to determine whether or not this particular measure before Parliament would affect the company. Mr. Préfontaine later that morning informed me that the company does not utilize this provision of the Act and furthermore has no intention of doing so even with these proposed amendments. As currently structured it has no use for the provision. It was made clear to me that it would make absolutely no sense for the company to pursue this course as it would require substantial reorganization and large costs with no corresponding benefit.

Furthermore, Wilson said, Martin had behaved properly in taking no active role in the preparation of clause 241 and in delegating responsibility for it to Secretary of State Peterson. Wilson criticized Martin only for not telling him in advance about the potential for apparent conflict of interest:

> I was not informed and I should have been. The department agrees with this. I have clearly established that in no way was Mr. Martin involved in the consideration of this issue, and all decisions were taken by the Secretary of State. There was therefore no real conflict of interest. Nonetheless, Mr. Martin sponsored this bill and questions have been raised by some members that this constitutes an apparent conflict of interest.
>
> Had I been informed in advance … there would have been a discussion on how best to handle the tabling of the bill under the name of the Minister of Finance, who is responsible for all tax legislation. It seems to me there would have been three choices: first, that Mr. Martin table the bill, as actually happened; second, we might have concluded that another minister should table the bill; and the third option would have been to have the minister table the bill but in the tabling include an explanatory note from the department explaining the background of these proposed amendments and the fact that it was a matter exclusively handled by the Secretary of State. On the basis of what I now know — that these amendments are only technical, that they have been under public discussion since 1995, the fact that it was a west coast organization that was seeking these clarifications, and the fact that the department had excluded the Minister of Finance from any involvement — I would have been led to the conclusion that the third option would have been the most appropriate in the circumstances.

Wilson's statement did not fully satisfy Loubier and the other opposition critics. They were especially uneasy with Wilson's acceptance at face value of the CSL officials' account of the impact of clause 241 on their company. All four opposition parties had asked for the establishment of a subcommittee to investigate the allegations; now Loubier moved a formal motion to this effect and it was defeated by the Liberal majority on the committee. And after that the controversy faded away, although the tension between business and politics inherent in Martin's position did not.

Up Against the Banks

One of the responsibilities that falls on the shoulders of the minister of finance is overseeing the major banks. In 1998, it was this aspect of his job that posed the most serious threat to Paul Martin's balancing act between the interests of business and the public interest. There would be winners and losers in the two proposed multibillion-dollar bank mergers announced in early 1998, and it was unlikely that Martin would be among the winners.

The difficulties inherent in Martin's responsibility for the banks were posed in stark terms in a survey that appeared in the April 1998 issue of the *Globe and Mail*'s *Report on Business Magazine*. This survey, an annual feature carried by the magazine, identified the Royal Bank of Canada as Canada's Most Respected Corporation in 1998. A serious-looking John Cleghorn, the Royal's chair and CEO, appeared on the cover. The other member banks of Canada's Big Five followed close behind on the Most Respected list: Bank of Montreal in fifth place, Canadian Imperial Bank of Commerce in seventh, Bank of Nova Scotia in tenth and Toronto-Dominion Bank in twelfth.

Winning the Most Respected prize has nothing to do with gaining the respect of the Canadian public; rather, the title is awarded on the basis of a poll of corporate CEOs. And *Report on Business Magazine* was not reticent about why the Royal Bank earned the favour of this select group: "It makes money like gangbusters. With assets of $245 billion and profits of $1.7 billion, it promises a long-term investment value that any CEO would adore."

In contrast to previous years, however, the 1998 survey did include a poll of the general public as well, analysed in a sidebar by marketing consultant John Dalla Costa. And results here were somewhat different from what they were in the poll of CEOs:

> Canadians and their CEOs are deeply divided about the country's Most Respected Corporations. While corporate leaders had a tough time choosing among 1997's top performers, the public at large had an even tougher time identifying any company to respect at all. Four in 10 Canadians drew blanks when asked to name a company that they admired.

According to Dalla Costa, Canadians were especially enthusiastic in their disrespect for the big banks:

> Few industries have struggled with the messy reality of relationship-building more than Canadian banks. At a time when many of the world's top banks are failing or struggling, Canada's banking industry has been getting stronger and generating record profits. Rather than winning admiration for their managerial moxie, banks have suffered loud disruptions in their annual meetings, public calls for ceilings on the executive pay of bankers and, more recently, firm resistance to the proposed merger of the Royal and Bank of Montreal.

> This is not a simplistic public antipathy toward corporate success. More fundamentally, the banks are reaping exactly the quality of respect that they have sown over the years in their relationships with customers.

In 1998, public attention on the banks focused primarily on the January announcement of the proposed Royal–Montreal merger, and then on the April announcement of a second merger, between CIBC and the Toronto-Dominion. Both mergers required approval from the federal government, and the elected official charged with representing the public interest in this matter was the minister of finance.

On one level, this was a role that Paul Martin could easily fit into. It was a natural for the MP who had insisted that the government had an important role in the economy and had forcefully criticized the Conservative government for its neglect of the environment — in other words, for the Paul Martin who had been virtually invisible since becoming minister of finance in 1993. And indeed, in his statements on the bank mergers, he sounded more like this older version of Paul Martin than he had in a very long time. Martin's frame of mind was not improved by the circumstance that he reportedly found out about the Royal–Montreal merger from the morning news rather than from the bankers involved, but most of his comments focused on the substance of the deals rather than on who knew what when.

Reacting to the announcement of the Royal–Montreal merger in January, he challenged the banks "to lower consumer charges, to guarantee that there will be no job loss, to guarantee that small and medium-sized business and that smaller towns in the country will benefit from this. That's the dare that I would put to them and that they should put to themselves." In March, commenting on the banks' contention that they needed the merger to protect their domestic market, he said, "I don't buy the rationale at all." He added, "I think the large institutions have an obligation and responsibility to the country, and I think part of that is that they don't do things that lead to massive dislocation and job loss."

Then in May, after the CIBC and TD had announced their proposed merger, Martin rejected the banks' argument that the reduction in competition the mergers would bring would be compensated for by foreign banks and new technology. "No country in the world has had foreign banks come in and open up extensive branching networks outside the major metropolitan centres," he said. Maintaining that it was important for small businesses and consumers in small towns to have competing bank branches, he evoked an even earlier Paul Martin, suggesting that the perspective from the banks' Toronto headquarters "is a very different perspective from Harrow, Ontario." The reference was to a small town near Windsor, in his father's old riding: "The bank branch is very important in towns like Harrow."

While Martin's performance as defender of the public interest won good reviews, there were many who felt that it was not entirely convincing. The Montreal *Gazette*'s perennially skeptical cartoonist Aislin had Martin's head on a rubber stamp with a big "OK" on the bottom. "But first, we'll be making some obligatory noise," said the head, while a voice in the corner commented, "It's called Martinizing." Business circles, by and large, agreed with Aislin, taking it for granted that the finance minister would not and could not block something that the banks wanted so passionately. Despite Martin's statements that the government would be looking closely at the mergers and determining whether they were in the public interest, *Report on Business Magazine* noted matter-of-factly that the Royal–Montreal merger "is expected to win government and regulatory approval." All the bluster notwithstanding, some observers had a hard time imagining that Martin and other key players in the cabinet were really blindsided by the mergers or actually opposed them. After all, Jean Chrétien was a member of the board of the Toronto-Dominion during his political hiatus, and most of the top bankers are friends and colleagues of Martin's. The chief lobbyist in Ottawa for the Royal and Montreal is a Liberal Party organizer, David MacNaughton.

The major Canadian banks with which Martin has become entangled are institutions that have long been at the very centre of Canadian economic life. Indeed, the presence of a Royal

Bank, CIBC or Scotiabank branch on a street corner is one of those reassuring sights that lets you know you are in Canada. At the same time, these banks have had an international component since the early years of their history. The Merchants' Bank of Halifax (which later became the Royal Bank of Canada) had a branch in Hamilton, Bermuda, before it had one in Montreal, and the Bank of Nova Scotia had a branch in Kingston, Jamaica, before it had one in Toronto. The Canadian banks spread especially through the Caribbean and Latin America but also to the United States, Europe and even as far afield as Vladivostok, where they briefly established branches on the heels of Canadian troops sent to suppress the Russian Revolution.

There was always a contradiction between the banks' international aspirations and the protected oligopoly situation they enjoyed in Canada, but as long as their international operations represented a relatively small proportion of their total business and banking in general remained largely confined within national boundaries, the contradiction was a manageable one. However, this had begun to change by 1963, when Finance Minister Walter Gordon met with the CEO of New York–based Citibank, James S. Rockefeller, to discuss Citibank's intention of taking over the Mercantile Bank of Canada, a small institution then controlled by Dutch interests. When one of Gordon's officials pointed out that the Canadian government could withdraw a bank's charter through the decennial revision of the Bank Act, Rockefeller noted in return that Canadian banks' licences to do business in New York State came up for renewal every year. Officers of several Canadian banks phoned Gordon to urge him not to do anything that would thwart Citibank's ambitions. Gordon's successor as finance minister, Mitchell Sharp, was open to the Rockefellers' ambitions, and the Mercantile became the subject of one of the classic Sharp–Gordon confrontations that marked the mid-1960s in Ottawa. The confrontation ended in an unsatisfactory compromise. Citibank did take over the Mercantile, but legislative restrictions were placed on its expansion.

The next revision of the Bank Act, in the 1970s, provided for a greater presence by foreign banks, although there were still limitations on the size and nature of their business. Meanwhile, the Royal, CIBC, Montreal, Scotiabank and T-D were evolving from being Canadian banks with a foreign presence to being international banks with a Canadian base. And financial markets increasingly transcended national borders, limiting the capacity of each individual government to carry out an autonomous monetary policy and driving the process that became known as globalization.

All of these tendencies have accelerated in the past two decades. And so, when the two big bank mergers were announced in 1998, international ambitions and international competition were at the heart of the rationale for them. "Size matters," John Cleghorn said, "because it allows us to make necessary investments in technology and to achieve the kind of scale that will make it possible to offer our customers better service and better value. It also will help Canada play a stronger role in international markets than it does today. And that in turn will mean better, more secure jobs for our employees as well as create rewards for our shareholders."

The Royal–Montreal combination would be a big bank for the twenty-first century, one that could roam the globe and, in Cleghorn's elegant words, "kick ass." The Bank of Montreal's Matthew Barrett adopted a more defensive analogy: They would not be like the local hardware store waiting for Home Depot to build a megastore on the corner. This is all well and good, but for Canadian banks to roam the globe, Canada would have to reciprocate and allow foreign banks to roam freely about Canada. If Canadian banks expect to be able to take equity positions in foreign banks, again there must be reciprocity. Furthermore, the reduction in competition involved in the shrinking of the Big Five to the Big Three can only be compensated for by an increased presence of foreign banks in Canada.

John Cleghorn's "kick ass" theory and Matthew Barrett's hardware store analogy were placed in perspective by the announcement of yet another major deal in the financial sector: the merger in the United States of Citicorp (the holding company that owns Citibank) and Travelers Group to form the world's largest financial services organization. Like their counterparts at the Royal and Montreal, the CEOs of both Citibank and Travelers took a defensive position: The merger was necessary to enable them to compete globally. If the new Royal–Montreal combination with assets of C$81 billion will now be able to kick global ass, what about the Citicorp–Travelers agglomeration with assets of more than US$698 billion? Big in banking is a very relative term.

Martin had a potential escape hatch from his bank-merger box in the form of the Task Force on the Future of the Canadian Financial Services Sector, appointed by the government with a wide-ranging mandate in December 1996. The question of mergers and acquisitions had already captured the task force's attention. In June 1997 two proposed takeovers — Scotia-bank's bid for National Trust and the Royal Bank's (ultimately unsuccessful) attempt to purchase London Life — prompted Secretary of State Jim Peterson to ask the task force for its views on such deals. A few weeks later the task force submitted a preliminary report to Peterson, concluding that there should be no general rule according to which "big shall not buy big," that mergers and acquisitions could be beneficial under some circumstances and should be considered on a case-by-case basis, and that there is significant competition in the financial services industry.

With its strongly business-oriented composition — chair Harold MacKay is a Regina corporate lawyer and director of several companies and vice-chair Pierre Ducros is a Montreal private investor — the task force did not reverse these conclusions in light of the much larger and more significant mergers announced in 1998. But it did soften them with some other observations and recommendations. In its September 1998 final report, it expressed skepticism about some of the reasons the banks had presented for the mergers, and it recommended that the minister of finance undertake a "public interest review process" before any merger is approved. With its on-the-one-hand-on-the-other-hand approach, the task force did not clearly point Martin in any particular direction. Once he made his decision, however, Martin could find support in its report for almost anything he wanted to do.

Other bodies were studying the mergers as well. There was another task force, this one made up of Liberal MPs, collecting views on the subject. And in July the government's Competition Bureau released the guidelines it would use in judging whether or not the mergers should be considered anticompetitive. The bureau would regard it as excessive concentration if any one bank were to have more than 35 per cent of the Canada-wide market for a given product, or if the top four banks were to have more than 65 per cent of the market. This concern would be mitigated if the bureau believed that new competitors or new technologies would provide the needed competition — a key argument put forward by the banks. However, it would use only a two-year time frame in judging these effects. The day after the Financial Services Task Force issued its report, a *Globe and Mail* analysis suggested that the government was now hoping that the Competition Bureau's final report, expected in December, would provide it with ammunition to take a tough stand against the mergers.

But with or without the help of the two task forces and the Competition Bureau, any conceivable stance Martin could take towards the bank mergers was fraught with political peril. If he vetoed the mergers, he risked having his business friends turn against him as they turned against John Turner over free trade in 1988. Turner's political career came to a quick end, and in such a scenario Martin's prospects would at the very least be severely damaged.

On the other hand, if he allowed the mergers to go through, he faced the formidable task of persuading Canadians that bank mergers were good for them. Otherwise he risked meeting the same fate as C.D. Howe, who in 1956 was too assiduous in his efforts to help his friends in the Texas oil industry gain approval for a natural gas pipeline. In the next year's federal election, Howe went down to personal defeat in his Port Arthur riding and the Liberal government he was part of lost to John Diefenbaker's Conservatives.

Of course, if anyone could convince Canadians of the merits of bank mergers, it was the politician who had talked them into accepting deep program cuts to eliminate the deficit. But in this case Martin's task was complicated by the fact that a negative attitude towards bank mergers was far from being limited to left-wing critics. Small business was generally opposed, and one of its leading representatives, Canadian Federation of Independent Business president Catherine Swift, said in January that "further concentration in the banking industry is not viewed as a positive development." Even someone as close to the heart of Canada's establishment as former Ontario lieutenant-governor and former National Trust head Hal Jackman didn't think much of the idea:

If you're in Goderich or Flesherton or something like that and you've got three bank branches and now you're going to have two, what do you care whether those big banks are big players in derivatives in New York or Switzerland? Canadian banks are becoming much more international and I think they run the risk of losing the concern for the people who built them.

Two independent-minded economists, Arthur Donner and former junior finance minister Doug Peters, issued a report in September suggesting that the bank mergers would cost thousands of jobs and should be blocked outright. Another critic was Peter Godsoe, chair and CEO of the Bank of Nova Scotia, the one major bank left without a merger partner. "Over all, there's no case for megamergers," Godsoe told the Liberal Caucus Task Force. "They're clearly anticompetitive, and we'd lose about one third of our banking system." And Conrad Black's Ottawa *Citizen*, while maintaining that the fate of the bank mergers should be "left to the market," picked apart the banks' rationale for the mergers. If Martin approved the mergers, no less than if he vetoed them, he risked alienating people who would normally be among his supporters.

This left a third option, perhaps the most likely one: to approve the mergers, but with conditions. Such an approach would only work, however, if the conditions were stringent enough to satisfy Canadians that their interests were being protected, but without vitiating the reasons the banks wanted to merge in the first place. One of the benefits corporations generally hope to derive from mergers is cost reduction, and more often than not this is achieved by cutting jobs. The banks denied that they had any such plans — indeed, Matthew Barrett insisted that the new Royal-Montreal combination would mean higher job levels and more branches.

In a report written for institutional investors and leaked in mid-August to the *Globe and Mail*, York University professor Fred Lazar sketched a picture of what Martin's conditions might look like: the sale of 11 per cent of the branches of the four banks involved, commitments to maintain job levels, a two-year freeze on service fees for retail banking, and specific dollar commitments for small business loans. Martin would also make it easier for foreign banks to gain entry and promote the creation of a unified Canada-wide credit union network. With these conditions, Lazar predicted, the mergers would be approved in April 1999.

Lazar's scenario is a credible one, and while the banks would undoubtedly grumble at such conditions they would probably swallow them in the end. But as of September, the banks had not succeeded in communicating a convincing case for the mergers, and political resistance appeared to be hardening.

Under these circumstances, any compromise Martin proposes, no matter how delicately crafted, will be difficult to sell.

The International Dimension

In almost any scenario, the further opening of the Canadian market to foreign banks will be a major result of the mergers. What is then to prevent the takeover of any and all Canadian banks — including the new Royal–Montreal and CIBC–TD combines? When this happens, what will remain of the ability of the Bank of Canada and federal government to set fiscal and monetary policy for this political entity we now know as Canada?

At the G7 meetings in Birmingham, England, in May 1998, Martin was one of the chief proponents of improving international supervision of the global financial system. In the wake of the turmoil in Asian markets, other finance ministers and heads of government were sympathetic to the idea. The finance ministers were mandated to come up with a detailed proposal to present to the leaders when they met again in 1999. This initiative represented a recognition that at this point effective regulation of the financial system needs to be transnational. Later the same month, Martin was also the spokesperson for the Asia-Pacific finance ministers in acknowledging that any measures to restructure Asian economies will need to take into account the impact on people as well as on financial institutions. In August he again pointed to the need for international financial supervision in a speech to the Couchiching Conference in Orillia, Ontario. He also suggested that international agreements that liberalize trade and investment need to be complemented by agreements that protect human rights and the environment and "restrain the commercial and financial excesses of the market." As with his tough statements in reaction to the bank mergers, he was sounding more like the Paul Martin of opposition days than the one Canadians had come to know in the four and a half years of his struggle against the deficit.

A more international perspective both comes naturally to Martin and suits him well at this point in his career. International affairs played a crucial role in the careers of two people who were among the strongest influences on him — his father and Maurice Strong. In the 1970s he was among the founders of the North-South Institute, an Ottawa-based research organization dealing with development issues. Furthermore, there has been an important international dimension to his work as finance minister. It was said of C.D. Howe in his prime that he ran everything except foreign affairs. With the whole shift of emphasis from the cold war diplomacy to global economics, Martin's portfolio includes foreign affairs. Martin acknowledged the international dimension of his responsibilities in his 1998 budget speech: "We would be making a very serious mistake if we ever came to believe that the global economy abroad means there is no role, no responsibility on the part of the government to provide opportunity and security at home." His subsequent statements represent a recognition that this role can itself only be carried out internationally. As he develops this position he is bound to come into conflict with the United States, which firmly believes in a strong governmental force in international trade and finance. It also believes this government oversight is already in place — in Washington.

The need for a transnational form of governance seems to become more obvious as the crisis in Japan sweeps through Asia, affecting other areas of the world as well, and as the anarchy in the former Soviet Union deepens. It was once the conventional wisdom that if small and medium-sized national economies were beyond the effective control of their national governments, the United States and Europe acting separately or in tandem could resolve any crisis — indeed could take advantage of any "foreign" crisis by forcing concessions from the afflicted area for American or German capital. This is being challenged now. For example, the American Federal Reserve cannot simply determine interest rates by conditions within the American continent. Now a slight but necessary rise in American interest rates could lead to the collapse of the monetary system in Asia and destroy the ruble. Martin may be only slightly ahead of his time in expressing the need for some global vehicle to try to save the market from itself — although it will probably take an international crisis to bring this to a boil.

And for Martin himself, a senior position in such an international authority (or an existing international body such as the World Bank) might be a more natural culmination to his career than the leadership of the Liberal Party and the prime ministership of Canada. Having closely watched his father's frustrations and been present at the humiliation of the 1968 leadership convention, he is intimately familiar with the futility of patiently waiting his turn. Having spent five years as finance minister in circumstances that demanded that he devote his considerable talents to pruning back rather than building up, he is also familiar with the limited room for manoeuvre available to national governments, and especially the government of Canada, in the era of trade agreements and global finance. The very meaning of sovereignty is undergoing revision: During Martin's time in office an international body, the World Trade Organization, effectively overturned an excise tax and other Canadian legislation designed to protect domestic magazines. Martin has had a privileged vantage point from which to see where real power is moving, and it is certainly not towards Ottawa. International power is the only possible effective curb on unilateral American power, and the need for such a curb may eventually come to be seen by the Americans themselves.

A Negative Achievement

Whether his career takes him to the leadership of the Liberal Party, to the international mandarinate, back to the private sector or into early retirement, Paul Martin's significance is secure. He is one of a small group of Canadian politicians who have had a lasting impact on the country without being party leaders — a group that includes Clifford Sifton, Ernest

Lapointe, C.D. Howe and Paul Martin, Sr. The one he most resembles is Howe, with his businessman's cast of mind applied to politics and his capacity for taking on a job and getting it done.

In comparison with his predecessors, however, Martin can claim only an essentially negative achievement. This achievement can be phrased in several ways. He cut back the apparatus of the federal state to restore it to fiscal health. He cut the deficit effectively, where the Tories did it ineffectively. Perhaps most profoundly, he ended the federal government's fifty-year centralizing thrust, reducing the financial presence of the federal government and its role in social programs and thus restoring the provinces to their proper place in the federation. Social progressives who defend Martin put his achievement in a somewhat different light: A more ideological minister would have cut more deeply, extensively and indiscriminately, perhaps even reducing taxes as the Harris government in Ontario did and necessitating even further cuts. But however it is cast, Martin's claim to have done great things in government rests on what he reduced, ended or prevented rather than on what he started or created. This is a reflection more on the times than on Martin. Whatever his personal inclinations, he recognized with that ancient pragmatist, the author of the Book of Ecclesiastes, that there is "a time to break down, and a time to build up."

From the time he entered politics and through his tenure as finance minister, Martin's business background and fiscal prudence have led many to portray him as a Liberal who would be at home in the Conservative or Reform party. The continuity between the Liberals' actions in office and those of the Tories who preceded them — cutbacks, free trade, the Goods and Services Tax — has been frequently pointed out. Some have even suggested that Martin's deficit-cutting program represented a betrayal of Liberal Party principles. This suggestion represents a misunderstanding not so much of Martin as of the Liberal Party. It is true that many of Canada's social programs, including the ones that Martin has weakened in pursuit of a balanced budget, were introduced by Liberal governments. But introducing these programs was as much a pragmatic response to a given situation — the rise of the CCF in the 1940s or the threat of the New Party (later the NDP) in the 1960s — as cutting them was for Martin.

Furthermore, there is nothing remotely strange or unnatural about the Liberals' having a close relationship with business and pursuing an agenda that business supports. Business was a strong presence in the King and Saint-Laurent governments, especially in the person of C.D. Howe, and even in the Pearson government, where ministers such as Mitchell Sharp and Robert Winters represented business concerns. The relationship between business and the Liberal Party became strained during the Trudeau era, and it fell apart completely at the time of the 1988 free trade election, when the Liberals under John Turner and the weight of Canadian business interests squared off on opposite sides of one of the crucial issues of the time. Chrétien and Martin have simply brought the relationship back to its historic norm.

But business is more demanding in its relations with government than it was in the expansive postwar era. It is no longer possible, as it was then, to develop and maintain a welfare state and keep business happy at the same time. We may yet see the emergence of an effective challenge to business's hegemony — one that will probably have to take place on an international scale. Until then, the negative achievements of a Paul Martin are the most that even a powerful cabinet minister can aspire to.

NOTE ON SOURCES

Paul Martin, Sr.'s own memoirs, published in two volumes under the title *A Very Public Life* (Toronto: Deneau, 1983–85), are the most extensive source for his political career. Memoirs of other Liberal politicians also provide insight into Martin and useful background on the workings of the Liberal Party, notably Keith Davey, *The Rainmaker: A Passion for Politics* (Toronto: Stoddart, 1986); Walter Gordon, *A Political Memoir* (Toronto: McClelland & Stewart, 1977); Tom Kent, *A Public Purpose* (Montreal/Kingston: McGill-Queen's University Press, 1988); and J.W. Pickersgill, *My Years with St. Laurent* (Toronto: University of Toronto Press, 1975). Other useful books on Liberal Party history include Robert Bothwell and William Kilbourn, *C.D. Howe: A Biography*; Richard Gwyn, *The 49th Paradox: Canada in North America* (Toronto: McClelland & Stewart, 1985); and Christina McCall Newman, *Grits: An Intimate Portrait of the Liberal Party* (Toronto: Macmillan, 1982).

For historical information on Canada Steamship Lines, an invaluable source was Edgar Andrew Collard, *Passage to the Sea: The Story of Canada Steamship Lines* (Toronto: Doubleday Canada, 1991). This book also provided useful data on the early years of Power Corporation of Canada. Another source on Canada Steamship Lines, in particular its most recent period, was *L'ère de la coeaupération* [sic], a slim but well illustrated volume published and distributed privately by CSL in 1995 to mark the 150th anniversary of the founding of its biggest and oldest predecessor company. Leaflets and news releases issued by CSL and Fednav provided information on their current activities, as did private conversations with individuals involved in the Montreal shipping scene.

Greg Weston, *Reign of Error: The Inside Story of John Turner's Troubled Leadership* (Toronto: McGraw Hill–Ryerson, 1988) gives the flavour of the Turner era. David Olive, "Paul Martin Jr., Shipping Magnate (And Next Leader of the Liberal Party)", *Canadian Business*, April 1984, is an interesting portrayal of Martin at the outset of his political career.

Martin's attack on the deficit and the struggles within the cabinet and the bureaucracy are recounted in detail in Edward Greenspon and Anthony Wilson-Smith, *Double Vision: The Inside Story of the Liberals in Power* (Toronto: Doubleday, 1996). Some of the same material is explored from a different point of view in Linda McQuaig, *The Cult of Impotence: Selling the Myth of Powerlessness in the Global Economy* (Toronto: Viking, 1998). Statistics on federal government debt and deficit levels came dirctly from the Department of Finance in Ottawa. Inflation figures were taken from the Statistics Canada website. Useful observations on Canada's productivity performance came from a 1994 Statistics Canada study entitled *Aggregate Productivity Measures* (cat. 15-204-XPE).

Newspapers (especially the Montreal *Gazette* and the *Globe and Mail*), Hansard, parliamentary committee reports and budget documents were used extensively throughout. The office of Yvan Loubier, MP (BQ—Saint-Hyacinthe–Bagot) provided useful information on the controversy surrounding Bill C-28. We thank Andrew Jackson, executive director of the Ottawa-based Centre for the Study of Living Standards, for his views on productivity and savings rates. We also thank economists Carl Beigie of McGill University; Michel Chossudovsky of the University of Ottawa; and Judith Maxwell, president of the Canadian Policy Research Networks; and political scientist Manfred Bienefeld of Carleton University for their views. Finally, we are indebted to political observers and people who have worked closely with Paul Martin who spoke to us off the record.

INDEX

Abbott, Douglas, 14, 18
Abitibi Consolidated, 49
Abitibi Price, 49
Adams, Nell. *See* Martin, Nell
Aislin, 148
Alberta, 131, 136
Alboim, Elly, 111
Algoma Steel Company, 33, 42
Allan, Sir Hugh, 39
anti-Semitism, 9
apprenticeship program, 89
Argus Corporation, 46-47
Asian financial crisis, 155
Atlantic Canada, 132
auto industry, 133-34
Auto Pact, 22
Axworthy, Lloyd, 86, 113-14
Aylmer Conference, 85, 86-87

Bank Act, 139, 149
Bank of Canada, 57, 84, 100, 101,
     121, 124
Bank of Montreal, 146, 150
Bank of Nova Scotia, 145, 150, 151
banks, 145-55
Banks, Hal, 42-44
Barber, John, 133
Barlow, Maude, 114
Barrett, Matthew, 150, 154
Bell Canada Enterprises, 49
Bennett, R.B., 14
Bienefeld, Manfred, 109
Bill 178, 73
Bill C-28, 138, 140-45
Bissonnette, André, 61
Black, Conrad, 46
Blake, Edward, 14
blind management agreement, 140
block funding, 113
Bloc Québécois, 54, 80, 90, 91, 103

bond-rating agencies, 106
Bothwell, Robert, 17
Bouchard, Lucien, 70, 78
Bourassa, Robert, 32, 67, 69
Brinco power company, 27
British Columbia, 100
Brundtland Report, 81
Bryce Commission, 46
budget secrecy, 110-11
business-government cooperation, 65,
     86

Cadieux, Marcel, 22
Caisse de Dépôt et Placement du
     Québec, 47, 65
Campagnolo, Iona, 75
Campbell, Bruce, 114
Campbell, Kim, 88
Canada Assistance Plan,
     113
Canada Development Investment
     Corporation, 139
Canada Health and Social Transfer,
     113-14
Canada Pension Plan contributions,
     129
Canada Steamship Lines (CSL), 32,
     33-59; Coverdale era, 40-41;
     debt, 57; early history, 38-40;
     labour and productivity problems,
     37; ocean shipping, 40, 41, 51;
     Power takeover of, 36; sale to
     Martin, 47-49; self-unloading
     bulk carriers, 51, 53, 54;
     shipyards, 37, 41-42, 44-45, 55;
     under McLagan, 42-44; under
     Martin's ownership, 50-55, 57-58
Canadian dollar, 69, 123-25, 126
Canadian Federation of Independent
     Business, 153

Canadian Imperial Bank of
    Commerce, 145, 147, 150
Canadian Pacific, 45-46, 47
Canadian Shipbuilding and
    Engineering, 57, 69
Canadian Steam Navigation Company,
    39
Canadian Vickers shipyard, 42
capital gains taxes, 98
Carstairs, Sharon, 73
Carter, Jimmy, 21
Cavelier, Robert, 63
CB Pak, 57
Charest, Jean, 78
Charlottetown Accord, 87-88
Chesterman, Tony, 57-58
child care, 89, 115
Chrétien, Jean, 60, 75, 76-77, 78,
    79-80, 81, 136-37, 148
Churchill, Winston, 23
cigarette tax, 139
Cimon, Éric, 91
Citibank, 22, 149-50
Citicorp, 151
Clarkson, Stephen, 26
Claxton, Brooke, 14, 18
Cleghorn, John, 145, 150
Collard, Edgar Andrew, 36, 38, 43
Collingwood shipyard, 55
Colonial Coach, 35
Competition Bureau, 151
Confederation of National Trade
    Unions, 37
conflict of interest issue, 138-45
Consolidated-Bathurst, 36, 37, 49
consumer price index, 104
Copps, Sheila, 74
corporate concentration, inquiry into.
    See Bryce Commission
corporate donations, 69, 90, 119-20
Côté, Marc-Yvan, 71
Couchiching Conference, 155
Courchene, Thomas J., 133
Coverdale, William H., 40
Cowan, Sheila (wife), 19
Cowan, William, 19
Coyne, James, 105
Croll, David, 8-9, 27
Crow, John, 57, 84, 100, 104, 105
CSL Equity Investments Limited, 53
CSL Group Inc., 49, 53, 140. See also
    Canada Steamship Lines

Dalla Costa, John, 146
Davey, Keith, 19, 21

Davie Shipbuilding, 37, 41, 44-45
debt, 89; at CSL, 57; charges, 96,
    99-100, 104; and deficit
    spending, 94-96; under Mulroney
    government, 97-103. See also
    deficit
deficit, 72, 92; elimination of, 109-14;
    government, 95, 110;
    Keynesianism, 97, 102; Ontario,
    131; Peterson government, 101;
    program cuts, 83, 111-14; Rae
    government, 101; Red Book, 90,
    107; reduction by spending, 83,
    93, 98-99; under Chrétien
    government, 115-18; under
    Mulroney government, 99-101.
    See also debt
de Grandpré, Jean, 26
Deniger, Pierre, 71
Desautels, Denis, 110
Desmarais, Louis, 32, 38
Desmarais, Paul, 32, 35-36, 37, 38,
    44-47, 49, 52
devolution, 129-34
Diefenbaker, John, 18, 43, 105
Dionne family, 10
Dodge, David, 108, 113
Dome Petroleum, 45
Dominion Glass, 37
Dominion Securities, 97
Dominion Stores, 46
Domtar, 46
Donner, Arthur, 153
downloading, 111, 129-32
downsizing, 44, 45
Drury family, 35
Duceppe, Gilles, 54, 81
Ducros, Pierre, 151
Dunn, Sir James, 42

Earnscliffe Strategy Group, 111
Earth Summit, 81
Eden, Anthony, 23
education, 127
Elder, Jim, 55, 57
election of 1957, 17-18
election of 1988, 66-70
election of 1993, 88-91
election of 1997, 119-20
election contrabutions. See corporate
    donations
Essex East riding, 8, 11
Established Programs Financing, 113
European Coal and Steel Community,
    34

Eves, Ernie, 134
exports, 127, 128

Famous Players, 9, 29, 139
Farber, Leonard, 141-42
Federal Commerce and Navigation
    Limited, 48
federalism, 76. *See also* devolution
Federal Reserve Board, 122-23, 156
Fednav Limited, 48, 49, 52-53, 57, 69
Fielding, W.S., 16
Filmon, Gary, 73, 79
Financial Services Task Force, 151-52
Fleming, William, 63
Ford strike, 9
Forget, Louis-Joseph, 39
Forget, Sir Rodolphe, 39
Fraser, Hohn, 61
Freeman, Don, 55
free market, 64-65
free trade, 22, 89, 132; election issue,
    66-70; and the environment, 82;
    Martin and, 64, 70-71; negotiated
    by King, 12
Friedman, Milton, 121

G7 meetings, 155
General Motors strike, 8-9
Ginn Publishing Canada, 139-40
globalization, 84-87, 150
Goar, Carol, 65
Godsoe, Peter, 153-54
Goldenberg, Eddie, 43
Goldenberg, H. Carl, 43
Goods and Services Tax, 89, 115-16
Gordon, Walter, 21, 22, 23, 24, 27,
    110, 149
government intervention, 65-66
Gray, Herb, 9
Great-West Life, 36
Great White Fleet, 40
Greenspan, Alan, 122
Greenspon, Edward, 108, 112
Gregg, Milton, 15
Grey, Deborah, 81
Gwyn, Richard, 129

Harper, Elijah, 79
Harris, Mike, 129, 130-34
Harrison Hot Springs Conference, 85
Hellyer, Paul, 24, 28, 118
Hepburn, Mitch, 8
Herle, David, 111

Hollinger Inc., 47
Hollinger Mines, 46, 47
Hŏsek, Chaviva, 87
Hotel Tadoussac, 41
Howe, C.D., 14, 17, 18, 27, 42, 92,
    135, 153, 156, 158
Hydro-Québec, 33
Hyndman, Stuart, 143

Imasco Corp., 57, 139
immigration, 122
Imperial Life, 36
Imperial Tobacco, 139
inflation, 100, 101, 104, 106
Inland Navigation Company, 39
Innes, Brian, 136
interest rates, high, 50, 57, 100, 106-7
International Labour Organization, 13
Investors' Group, 36
Iron Ore Company of Canada, 51

Jackman, Hal, 153
James Richardson and Sons, 33
Japan, 86
Johnson, Daniel, 26, 32
Johnson, Lyndon, 21
Johnston, Donald, 62

Kennedy, John F., 21
Kent, Tom, 20-21
Keynesianism, 94-97
Kierans, Eric, 114
Kilbourn, William, 17
King, Mackenzie, 7, 11, 14, 28; free
    trade with US, 12;
    international affairs, 13; and New
    Deal, 14; retirement, 16
Kingston Conference, 19-21, 85
Kingsway Transport, 40, 50, 55
Kolber, Leo, 69

labour costs, 126
labour movement, 9-10, 20, 45, 121
La Compagnie du Richelieu, 38-39
Lafontaine, Louis, 16
Lake Carriers' Association, 43
Lalonde, Marc, 75
LaMarsh, Judy, 27
Lanthier, Claude, 62, 66, 70
Lapierre, Jean, 75, 80
Lapointe, Ernest, 16, 158
La Presse, 36, 45

LaSalle-Émard riding, 62-63, 67, 69, 70, 90, 91
Laurentide Financial Corporation, 36
Laurier, Wilfrid, 7, 12
Lazar, Fred, 154
Lemay, Raymond, 50
leveraged buyouts (LBOs), 44-45
Lévesque Beaubien Geoffrion, 90
Lewis, David, 137
Liberal Party: 7, 158-59; 1990 leadership convention, 72, 76, 79-80; centralism, 86; electoral support in Quebec, 67, 136-37; ideological division, 15, 21-22; leadership succession, 14-15 28; and Meech Lake Accord, 74, 76-80; in opposition (1957-63), 19-21; relationship with business, 68-69, 83-84; right wing, 26-27; thinkers' conferences, 85-87; under Chrétien, 136-37; under King-Saint-Laurent, 136; under Pearson-Trudeau, 136
London Life, 151
Loubier, Yvan, 138, 141, 145
Luce, Henry, 12

Maastricht Treaty, 90
McCain Foods, 90
McCall, Christina, 10, 26
McConnell, J.W., 36, 42
Macdonald, John A., 14, 133
McDonald, Marci, 139, 140
McDougald, Bud, 46
MacEachen, Allan, 24
MacKay, Harold, 151
McKenna, Frank, 73, 74, 79
Mackenzie, Alexander, 14
MacLaren, Roy, 84
Maclean Hunter, 69
McLellan, Anne, 112, 136
MacNaughton, David, 148
McQuaig, Linda, 108
Mahoney, William, 20
Malépart, Jean-Claude, 81
Manitoba, 73, 74
Manley, John, 84, 140
Manning, Preston, 81, 88
Manoir Richelieu, 41
Manufacturers Life Insurance, 57, 138
Marchand, Jean, 26
Marchi, Sergio, 112
Marine Industries, 45
Martin, Mary-Ann (sister), 8, 11
Martin, Nell (mother), 8, 11, 93

Martin, Paul, Jr., 44; birth, 8; early business career, 34-38; entry into politics, 60-66; environmental critic, 80-83; and father's leadership bid, 24, 28-29; finance portfolio, 93, 103-14; international affairs, 155-57; leadership candidacy, 71,76-80; marriage, 19; personal fortune, 56; polio attack, 10; political fortunes, 135-38; president of CSL, 37; pro-business stance, 82-83; purchase of CSL, 47-49; rookie MP, 71-72; student days, 10-11, 19
Martin, Paul, Sr. (father): cabinet minister, 10; constituency politician, 10-11; interest in politics, 7-8; international affairs, 13; labour ties, 9-10; leadership succession, 14-16, 23-24; left Liberalism of, 13-14; marriage, 8; minister of external affairs, 22-23; party leadership bid, 7, 24-29; retirement, 29-30; and socialism, 9
Massé, Marcel, 112
Massey-Ferguson, 46
Massey, Vincent, 14
Matt Shipyard, 69
Mazankowski, Don, 103
Meech Lake Accord, 66, 72-80, 136
Mercantile Bank of Canada, 22, 149-50
Merchants' Bank of Halifax, 149
mergers, bank, 147-55
M.F. Strong Management Limited, 34
Michael Wilson, 97-98
Millennium Scholarship Fund, 111, 114, 127, 130
monetary policy, 102. See also Bank of Canada
Montreal Trust, 36, 49
Moody's, 106
Morden, Grant, 39-40
Mulroney, Brian, 32, 51, 79, 136
Munro, Ross, 15, 16
Murray, Lowell, 79

Nathanson, Paul, 9, 29, 139
National Action Committee on the Status of Women, 87, 88
National Council on Welfare, 114
National Policy, 133
National Trust, 151

NATO, 17
Nellmart, 139
Nesbitt, A.J., 33
Nesbitt, Thomson and Company
    Limited, 33, 40
New Brunswick, 73, 74
New Deal, 10, 13-14, 95
New Democratic Party (NDP), 20, 87,
    132, 134
Newfoundland, 74, 78
Newman, Peter C., 19, 45
Nicholson, Peter, 108, 125, 126
Nixon, Bob, 137
Nixon, Harry, 137
Non-Accelerating Inflationary Rate
    (NAIRU), 120-21
NORAD, 17
Norcen Energy Resources Limited, 34
Noronic, 33, 42
Norris, Thomas, 43, 44
North American Free Trade
    Agreement, 89. *See also* free trade
Northern Navigation Company, 39
North-South Institute, 156
"notwithstanding clause", 73

Oerlikon Aerospace, 61, 69
oil prices, 96
old-age pensions, 114. *See also*
    personal benefits
Olive, David, 28, 44
Ontario, 101, 107, 129, 130-34, 136-37;
Ontario Hydro, 13
Ottawa Citizen, 154

Paramount Communications, 139-40
Parisien, Jean, 35
Passage Holdings, 53, 140
Pathy, Laurence, 48-49, 52
Pawley, Howad, 73
Pearson, Lester, 14, 16, 18, 25
Peckford, Brian, 74
Pépin, Jean-Luc, 32
Perception Analyzer, 111
personal benefits, indexation of, 96,
    98-99
personal income taxes, de-indexing, 96
Peters, Doug, 108, 141, 153
Peterson, James, 141, 144, 151
Petro-Canada, 32
pipeline debate, 17, 153
Pitre, Fred, 53
Polymer, 92
Polysar, 69

Power Corporation: interest in Canadian
    Pacific, 47; leveraged buyouts,
    44-50; sale of Canada Steamship
    Lines, 47; takeover bid for Argus,
    46; Trans-Canada takeover of, 35
Powerpoint, 111
Préfontaine, Pierre, 143
Prenor, 69
productivity, economic, 125-28
Progressive Conservative Party, 61,
    64-65, 87
Provincial Transport Limited, 35, 36

Quebec, 24, 45, 73, 107, 136-137;
    federal election of 1988, 69;
    federal election of 1993, 90; and
    free trade, 64, 69-70; indigenous
    business class, 65; and Meech
    Lake Accord, 72, 78
Quebec Steamship Company, 40
Quebec Stock Savings Plans, 65

Rae, Bob, 33, 101, 130
Rae, John, 32
Rand formula, 9
Reagan, Ronald, 21
Rebick, Judy, 88
recession, 84, 100, 101
Red Book, 88-90
Redpath Industries, 57, 69
Redpath Sugar, 90
Reform Party, 81, 88, 107
revenues, federal, 109
reverse takeover, 35, 36
Richelieu and Ontario Navigation
    Company, 38, 39
Riley, Susan, 61
Robinson, Michael, 75
Rocheleau, Gilles, 75, 80
Rochette, Louis, 44-45
Rock, Allan, 136
Rockefeller, James S., 149
Romanow, Roy, 130
Ronning, Chester, 22-23
Roosevelt, Franklin D., 12, 13
Roosevelt, James, 13
Royal Bank of Canada, 97, 139, 145,
    146, 149, 150, 151

Saint-Laurent, Louis, 28; successor to
    King, 14-17; and Suez crisis, 17;
    and US foreign policy, 12-13,
    16-17

St. Lawrence Seaway, 41
St. Michael's College, 19
Sault Ste. Marie, 77
Sauvé, Maurice, 32
savings, personal, 128-29
Schefferville, 51
Seafarers' International Union, 42-43
self-unloading bulk carriers, 51, 53, 54
Sharp, Mitchell, 20, 24, 27, 140, 149
shipping industry: Bill C-28 and,
    141-45; difficulties, 50-51;
    secrecy, 48-49
Sifton, Clifford, 157
Simpson, Jeffrey, 95
Sincennes, Jacques, 38
social Liberalism, 13-14, 21, 85
Southam Inc., 47
"stagflation" 96
Standard & Poor's, 106
Standard Broadcasting, 46
Stanfield, Robert, 24
Starr, Michael, 140
Steel Company of Canada, 50
steel industry, 50-51
Stevens, Sinclair, 61
Stewart, Jane, 137
Stinson, William, 69
stock market crash of 1987, 100
Stone Container, 49
Strong, Maurice, 32-35, 60, 61
supply-side economics, 97
sustainable development, 82, 89
Swain, Harry, 112
Swift, Catherine, 153

tainted blood compensation, 114
tax cuts, 129, 131-32
Taylor, Len, 82
Telmer, Colin R., 133
Thiessen, Gordon, 105
Thomson, P.A., 33
Thomson, Peter N., 35
Thunder Bay, 77
Thurow, Lester, 85, 86
Tobin, Brian, 136
Tobin Tax, 90
Toronto-Dominion Bank, 145, 147,
    150

Trans-Canada Airlines, 92
Trans-Canada Corporation Fund, 35
Travelers Group, 151
Trudeau, Pierre, 25-29, 46, 78, 79, 136
Turner, John, 24, 60, 61; and deficit,
    95-96; and free trade, 68;
    leadership questioned, 66-67
Turner, William, 37

ULS International, 55
underemployment, 127
unemployment, 89, 100, 101, 104,
    120-23
Unemployment Insurance, 114
United Auto Workers, 8, 9
United Nations, 13
United States, 156; economic
    productivity, 126; free trade with,
    12; investments in Canada, 21;
    market, 52, 128; unemployment
    rates, 120, 122; Vietnam, 22-23

Varity, 46-47
Veliotis, Takis, 37
Verolme shipyard, 54
Via Rail, 56, 102, 141
Vietnam, 22-23
Voyageur bus line, 55-56, 141.
    See also Provincial Transport
    Limited

wages, 126
Wagner Act, 9
Walkon, Tom, 132
Webster, Lorne, 69
Wells, Clyde, 74, 79, 80
Wilson, Howard, 140, 141, 143-44
Wilson, Michael, 97-98, 102, 110,
    111, 112
Wilson-Smith, Anthony, 108, 112
Winters, Robert, 27, 28
World Bank, 157
World Trade Organization, 157

Young, Doug, 116-17